Contents

		page
	Introduction, by John Thomas	5
I	THE FORTH—RIVER AND FIRTH	7
II	HIGH DAYS AND HOLIDAYS (1854–1880)	15
III	THE EXCURSION HEYDAY (1881–1898)	29
IV	THE RAILWAY FERRIES	47
V	TWENTIETH-CENTURY DEVELOPMENTS (1898–1918)	60
VI	TWILIGHT INTERLUDE (1919–1945)	81
VII	THE FINAL FLING (1946–1969)	94
VIII	FORTH OCCASIONS	107
IX	MACHINERY	121

APPENDICES

1	Steamboat liveries	131
2	NBR steamers 1888 (Suitability for use as gunboats)	135
3	Vessels used on 'View the Fleet' Excursions, 1860	136
4	*Carrick Castle* summer programme 1884	139
5	Galloway Saloon Steam Packet Company: Sailings for week-ending 15 August 1897	141
6	David Wilson and Sons, Holiday Sailings 1906	144

FLEET LISTS	145
BIBLIOGRAPHY	164
AUTHOR'S NOTES AND ACKNOWLEDGEMENTS	165
INDEX	167

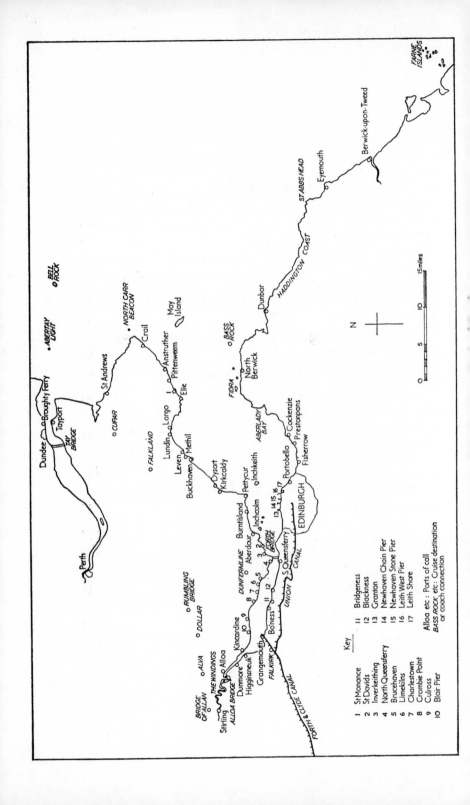

Key

1 St Monance
2 St Davids
3 Inverkeithing
4 North Queensferry
5 Brucehaven
6 Limekilns
7 Charlestown
8 Crombie Point
9 Culross
10 Blair Pier

11 Bridgeness
12 Blackness
13 Granton
14 Newhaven Chain Pier
15 Newhaven Stone Pier
16 Leith West Pier
17 Leith Shore

Alloa etc : Ports of call
BASS ROCK etc : Cruise destination
or coach connection

Introduction
by John Thomas

In 1812 Henry Bell with his *Comet* pioneered a long line of Clyde excursion steamers. It is not so well known that in 1813 Henry Bell with the same *Comet* pioneered a long line of Forth excursion steamers.

Bell as a youth had worked for the Bo'ness shipbuilding firm of Shaw and Hart. When his *Comet* required an overhaul he sailed her through the Forth and Clyde Canal and entrusted her to his old employer. It was while he was on the Forth that he put his vessel on an excursion run from Bo'ness to Leith at a single fare of 7s 6d. The *Edinburgh Courant* of 21 May commented, 'The Comet of Helensburgh, a vessel worked by steam and the first of the kind ever seen in this quarter, is at present lying in Leith harbour.'

An extensive literature has grown up round the Clyde steamers. The Forth boats have remained unsung—until now.

The Forth from its source in western Perthshire to the mouth of its estuary is 116 miles long, and of that distance the 63½ miles from Stirling to the sea were navigated by excursion steamers. The vessels called at no fewer than 63 piers.

The Forth takes 12½ miles to cover the 6½ miles between Stirling and Alloa. These are the Windings, the incredible loops into which the river twists itself in traversing the flat carseland. At Alloa the channel is a quarter of a mile wide, at Kincardine it is half a mile wide. Then it balloons to 3 miles at Bo'ness only to narrow again to 1¼ miles at Queensferry. There the river merges into the estuary, which funnels out until, at its mouth, the opposite shores are 17½ miles apart.

Until engineers learned to bridge wide expanses of water the Forth was a formidable barrier to north and south traffic. It was natural that the first ships to ply on its waters should be ferry boats. Some of the ferries are ancient. The Queensferry Passage operated from the reign of Queen Margaret of Scotland until the opening of the Forth road bridge—800 years.

5

With the coming of the steam age, towage firms sent steam tugs to patrol the Forth approaches ready to take arriving sailing ships to berths at Leith, Newhaven and other river ports. In the intervals of waiting for trade the owners found it profitable to take their vessels into port and embark passengers for short pleasure trips. Some owners kept a tug specially spruced up for this duty. From this situation there emerged the Forth excursion tug properly equipped and certificated for the job. And when trade had developed sufficiently there came the Clyde-style excursion steamer.

The Clyde dynasties of shipowners—Campbell, Williamson and Buchanan—were matched on the Forth by MacGregor, Jamieson and Galloway. The Forth had its share of rivalry and racing. The flamboyant George Jamieson would have held his own with any Clyde skipper. His red-hulled *Fiery Cross*, which traditionally crossed the Forth on her last run of the season with a tarred, wooden cross blazing at the stern, certainly lacked nothing in character.

Mr Brodie takes us on many vessels to many destinations. We sail upriver to Stirling, 'shooting' the Alloa railway bridge in the process and using independently-worked paddles to navigate the Windings. We sail round the islands of the Forth and embark on adventurous voyages out into the German Ocean. We find out what happened to the Clyde favourite *Redgauntlet* when she encountered the short, steep seas of the Forth Estuary. We join the holiday crowds packing the Aberdour steamers. We go with the excursionists on a sea bird shooting trip when the ship's boat was launched to pick up the 'bag', and are with the passengers who boarded an excursion steamer which joined ships of the Royal Navy during the *live* bombardment of an old fort on a Forth island. We accompany Professor Albert in his attempt to swim the Forth. We make the acquaintance of *Lord Elgin* and *Lord Mar* built in 1876 with compound diagonal engines, a type not seen on the Clyde for another 23 years; to say nothing of *Electric Arc* the world's first electrically propelled vessel.

Mr Brodie takes up his story in 1854 when the excursion tug was well established, the first true excursion steamer was about to emerge, and interesting things were happening to the ferries. But first he sets the scene by describing the peculiar hazards which faced steamboat operators on the Forth.

Chapter I

The Forth—River and Firth

THE TIDE

Tidal conditions in the Forth made it impossible to operate the precision, railway-style timetables familiar to users of the Clyde steamers. Unlike the Clyde with its low tidal range and slow-moving water, the Forth was subject to a tidal range of twenty feet in places. All the old harbours dried out at low water so that it was necessary to ferry passengers ashore using what on the Forth were called 'flory' boats. Sandbanks and large boulders which shifted position in spates were further hazards.

The Merchant Shipping Act of 1855, in laying down the conditions for carrying passengers on steamships, specified calm water (Class 5 certificate) as existing above Queensferry, and moderately calm water (Class 4 certificate) as existing inside a line drawn from Portobello to Kirkcaldy. Beyond that limit was the open sea where a Class 3 certificate was required for daylight summertime excursions. Year-round operations in the outer waters required a full home trade Class 2 certificate.

The constrictions of the river posed problems. When the flood passes Queensferry, it develops whirls towards the shores and for the first hour, while the tide is flowing in mid-stream, it is still ebbing at the sides! Above Grangemouth there is a reverse flow known as the 'lek'. The flood tide almost reaches high water mark in four hours and then suddenly reverses direction, leaking out for the next hour or more. This is followed by the second flood which ultimately reaches the high water mark. The 'lek' and the second flood are gentle compared with the first which travels at some speed.

The ebb is very fast and rips through the Windings at twelve to fourteen knots, but reduces to eight by the time it reaches

Queensferry. Its maximum velocity is in the main channel where it does a good dredging job. Along the shores it is slower, but even so, calls between Alloa and Queensferry were difficult, and if mooring ropes were not caught first throw it was a struggle to get the ship back to the pier. Where florying was necessary the engines had to be kept running astern to hold the ship in position. The ebb lasts just over four hours, and below Grangemouth is followed by the long period of slack water common to the firth. Further up river the 'lek' runs in for about an hour, raising the water level two feet at spring tides at Kincardine, and is followed by a second slower ebb.

The river steamships made skilful use of these tides. The 'Stirling Steamboat' was advertised in 1814 to leave Stirling 'at the hour of high water at Leith' and took seven hours for the journey. In other words she left Stirling assisted by the last of the 'lek', but for the greater part of the voyage through the Windings steamed into the second flood. Just before Alloa the ebb caught her and assisted her to about Bo'ness, leaving her to paddle through slack water to her destination. The return voyage, leaving Newhaven two hours before low water, followed a similar pattern—slack water to Bo'ness, flood to beyond Alloa, the Windings tackled against the 'lek' and Stirling being reached on the early part of the second flood.

Later more powerful vessels did the journey in three hours, but the pattern of steaming through the Windings against a slight tide and of using tidal assistance between the Alloa bridge and Queensferry, was used whenever possible. Under these conditions there is ample water in the Windings, which then resemble the Norfolk Broads. In early years the 'fords of Stirling' constituted a hazard and with the larger ships of later years, the slightest deviation from the channel resulted in grounding in soft mud. Such groundings were commonplace and caused no concern. With the reverse tide, and a jab astern on the engine, the ship floated off safely.

The Queensferry Passage vessels also had to struggle with the tide. Until 1964 when the service ceased, all vessels ran with three black balls permanently fixed to their signal lanyard, signifying 'Keep clear; I am out of control.' The later vessels had ample power in normal conditions but the early ships could not steer a straight course in mid-stream. For this reason there

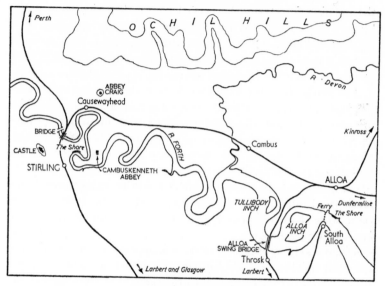

Map of the Windings

were alternative piers on the south shore and the steamer made for whichever it could reach most easily.

The Hawes, or Newhalls pier was the coach connection point and, at slack high water, the ferry ran direct to it from North Queensferry. At ebb-tide the ship was swept down river, landing at Longcraig below the railway bridge. There it manoeuvred and then crawled up to Newhalls where it loaded and unloaded before continuing up-river to Port Edgar. It turned at the pier there and steamed out across the river, hoping to reach North Queensferry before being swept out to sea. At flood tide this route was reversed. By the 1880s the ferry was sufficiently powerful usually to make a direct passage and this was of some importance as an unanticipated diversion could lead to a nasty collision with the railway bridge.

The Alloa Bridge

A hazard closely associated with the tide was the 'shooting' of the railway swing bridge a mile and half above Alloa. Sixty feet wide, the opening for steamers was little more than the beam of the biggest ships across the paddleboxes, and cross currents ran at up to 5–6 knots. The only way the ship could steer a steady course was to maintain full engine speed. With a tide behind, it could approach the bridge at speeds of up to 25mph.

The bridge lay on a bend in the river and was no higher than the surrounding countryside. If a train was crossing, the bridge operator would not hear a steamer siren, and might have as little as one minute's visual warning of its approach. It was impossible to open the bridge in this time. These circumstances were too dangerous for the Galloway company's boats to rely on the span opening and all the vessels were fitted with hinged masts and telescopic funnels, allowing them to pass under the bridge without requesting it to be opened. (The passenger tugs always waited for it to be opened.)

When a ship approached there was activity on the foredeck as the mast was lowered and brought down over the bows, where it projected like a long bowsprit. At the same time, the engine-room staff were telescoping the funnel by means of a rack and pinion controlled by chain from a handle or winch in the boiler room. When elevated the funnel tended to wobble and four taut stays, which sagged as the funnel was lowered, held it in position. The process of getting ready to 'shoot' the bridge took about five minutes. Once the funnel was down, the ship's bridge and after-deck were smothered in choking smoke and it must have been difficult for the captain to see where his ship was going.

The Alloa bridge was closed to rail traffic in the 1960s, with the swing span left open for almost non-existent river traffic and was demolished in 1971–2.

The Edinburgh Shore

The Forth steamers derived most of their traffic from Edinburgh and its environs. The ports and piers on the Edinburgh shore were therefore of great importance to the operating companies.

Leith, the principal port of Edinburgh, was not at first suitable for regular passenger sailings. It was not until a sandbar was dredged and the West Pier opened in 1852 that Leith became the main starting point for the passenger steamers. In the early days

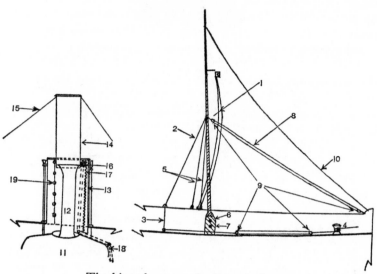

The hinged mast and telescopic funnel

KEY

1	Lamp hoist	**9**	Sheaf blocks	**15**	Stays
2	Back stay	**10**	Top fore stay	**16**	Pinion
3	Lowering hawser	**11**	Boiler casing	**17**	Rack
4	Winch	**12**	Flue (inner funnel)	**18**	Control chains
5	Side stays	**13**	Outer lower funnel	**19**	Steady guides
6	Securing pin				
7	Hinge pin	**14**	Upper funnel		
8	Lower fore stay				

Procedure for lowering the mast

Any signals being flown, or lamps being carried are first removed from the hoist (**1**). The back stays (**2**) are then detached from the bulwarks, and fastened to hawsers (**3**) which run forward through guides along each side of the ship, through a set of sheaf blocks, on to a bollard or round the winch (**4**). The side stays (**5**) are then detached, and the securing pin (**6**) removed from the mast. The lower fore stay (**8**) is then pulled through its sheaf blocks (**9**) until the mast is vertical, held in place only by the pull of the back stays. These are then slowly released, lowering the mast until it lies across the bows of the ship.

STEAM  CONVEYANCE

BETWEEN

EDINBURGH, ALLOA, and STIRLING,

BY THE

PRINCE OF WALES & ALBERT STEAMERS.

LANDING and Embarking Passengers (casualties excepted) at NORTH QUEENSFERRY, BO'NESS, CHARLESTON, CROMBIEPOINT, KINCARDINE, and DUNMORE.

Fares.—From Granton Pier to Stirling. Cabin 2s.; Steerage 1s. 4d. Granton Pier to Alloa. Cabin 1s. 6d.: Steerage 1s.

Day Tickets issued for going and returning same day.

Granton Pier to Stirling. Cabin 3s.; Steerage 2s. Granton Pier to Alloa. Cabin 2s. 6d.; Steerage 1s. 6d. Intermediate Ports in Proportion.

A PLEASURE TRIP ONCE A WEEK

From STIRLING to GRANTON, and GRANTON to STIRLING, calling at Intermediate Ports. Cabin 1s.; Steerage, 6d. Same Fare charged in returning.

Tourists desiring to enjoy a treat, are respectfully recommended to go by the above Steamers, and view the beautiful scenery on the banks of the Forth. It is one of the finest sails in Scotland. Many parties avail themselves of this interesting and cheap route in travelling between Edinburgh and Glasgow, by Steamers from Granton Peir to Stirling, thence per Scottish Central Railway to Glasgow, and *vice versa.*

Information as to hours of sailing, &c., to be had in Edinburgh, at Croall's Coach Office, No. 10, Princes Street, and MURRAY'S TIME TABLE OFFICE, 69, George Street, and at the Edinburgh, Leith, and Granton Railway Station, North Bridge Street (whence Passengers are conveyed to Granton Pier for the Steamers)—in Glasgow at the Star Hotel, and at Wordie and M'Arthur's, 120, Brunswick Street, and Madeira Court, 251, Argyle Street.

N.B.—*The Daily Sailings of these Steamers are advertised regularly in the Company's Bill's, which are printed every fortnight.*

Stirling, 1851. **ANDREW DRUMMOND.**

NOTICE TO PASSENGERS

BETWEEN THE

Chain Pier, Newhaven, and Kirkaldy, Dysart, Leven & Largo.

For particulars, apply at "THE BOX," late the Duty-House, and MURRAYS' TIME TABLE OFFICE, 69, George Street, Edinburgh; 47, Bernard Street, Leith; or here, to .

ANDREW GREIG.

Chain Pier, July 1851.

Steamer companies' announcements of 1851

of steamboats Newhaven was the favoured packet station. The Newhaven Chain Pier built in 1821 had a one-berth landing stage 500ft from the shore and connected to the shore by a suspension bridge supported by four wooden towers. For twenty years the Chain Pier was the focal point of the Forth services. Following its purchase in 1840 by Andrew Greig it was used mainly by his own steamers, the other traffic having moved to Leith or Granton. The Chain Pier was used as a sea bathing station until it was destroyed in a gale in 1898.

At Granton, further west, a passenger and cargo pier was opened in June 1838. Capable of taking vessels at all states of the tide, its main function was to serve the Granton–Burntisland ferry. But as accommodation increased the Forth fleets based themselves on Granton. It was only after its rise as an extremely busy railway ferry terminal that the excursion steamers deserted it in favour of the new facilities at Leith.

The Clyde introduced its first integrated rail and steamboat service in 1841 with the opening of the Glasgow, Paisley & Greenock Railway. But five years before that the horse-hauled trains of the Edinburgh & Dalkeith Railway had connected at Fisherrow with *Morning Star* of the Musselburgh & Fisherrow Steam Packet Company for cruises to Dunbar, Eyemouth and Berwick and excursions round the Bass Rock. Many years later a pleasure pier in the English style was opened at Portobello three miles east of Edinburgh. Its eventful story is told in these pages.

The following list of ports served gives some idea of the range and scope of the Forth sailings.

Forth Ports of Call

Edinburgh & Environs

Granton
Newhaven, Chain Pier
Newhaven, Stone Pier
Leith, Shore
Leith, West Pier

Leith, Victoria Wharf
Leith, Tourist Steamer Terminal
Portobello
Musselburgh, Fisherrow

The River
West Lothian

South Queensferry, Longcraig pier

South Queensferry, Hawes pier

13

The River
West Lothian—cont.
South Queensferry, Town pier
South Queensferry, Galloway pier
South Queensferry, Port Edgar
Blackness, Castle pier
Bridgeness
Bo'ness

Stirlingshire
Grangemouth
Higginsneuk
Dunmore
South Alloa
Stirling

Clackmannan
Alloa, Shore
Alloa, Ferry Slip

Fife
Kincardine
Blair Pier
Culross
Crombie Point
Charlestown
Limekilns
Brucehaven
North Queensferry, Railway Pier
North Queensferry, Town pier

The Firth
Fife
Inverkeithing
St David's
Aberdour, Stone Pier
Aberdour, Hawkcraig Pier
Burntisland
Pettycur
Kirkcaldy
Dysart
Buckhaven
Methil
Leven
Lundin Beach
Largo
Elie
St Monance
Pittenweem
Crail
St Andrews
Tayport

Angus
Dundee, West Protection Wall

Perth
Perth, South Inch

East Lothian
Prestonpans, Morrison's Haven
Cockenzie
North Berwick
Dunbar

Berwickshire
Eyemouth

Northumberland
Berwick-upon-Tweed

Islands
Inchcolm
Inchkeith
May Island

Chapter II

High Days and Holidays
1854—1880

MacGregor & Galloway

By the mid-eighteenth century excursion boats had been operating on the Forth for nearly forty years. The services, however, had been spasmodic and were given mainly when tugs could be spared from their normal duties. Most of the vessels were Tyne-built and many of their owners and masters were Tynesiders. Ralph Stoker was one such man. He chartered his vessels to local men. In 1859 *Stokers* was advertised for 'pleasure and excursion parties' and was popularly employed on works outings and on cruises to Kirkcaldy.

It was not until 1854 that the excursion business was put on a solid fleet basis. In that year Donald R. MacGregor, a Leith insurance broker and merchant, formed a partnership with Captain John Galloway, a former Leith shipmaster, to finance a towing and excursion business. They started off with the tug *Carrs* and sailed her all that first summer from the West Pier at Leith on morning and evening trips to Aberdour and Inverkeithing, and afternoon cruises to Inchcolm. In August they purchased the rights to the ancient Kirkcaldy ferry and placed *Goliah* on a run via that port to Leven and Largo. After a winter lapse *Alma* restarted the service running only to Kirkcaldy and Dysart but traffic was light and on 29 June 1855 the service was abandoned.

Thereafter the partners concentrated on the Aberdour passage, the tug *Alma* opening the season on 30 June. By the autumn of 1856 the Saturday Half Holiday Association was offering round trips from Leith to Aberdour by the MacGregor boat (not landing) at single fare. In 1857 fares were cut to 1d on weekdays and 4d on Saturdays—this for a 13-mile round trip.

Lord Morton, the proprietor of Aberdour, helped the partners by leasing land at the village for summer dwellings. The one time quarrying village developed into a popular summer resort and ensured the success of the excursion tug. From 1858 the Aberdour passage was direct at fares of 9d cabin, 6d steerage (passengers not landing paying only a single fare). During the next decade the following steamers were advertised:

1854	*Carrs*
1855–6	*Alma*
1857	*Alma* or *Energy*
1858–9	*Xantho*
1860	*Pilot*
1861	*Blue Bonnet, Alma* or *Goliah*
1862	*Ruby*
1863–4	*Robert Scott*
1865	*Pearl*

All were tugs with the exception of *Xantho*, the former Anstruther packet vessel. Throughout the period there were frequent calls at Inchcolm and occasional excursions to Kirkcaldy or Inverkeithing.

Competition was provided in 1865 by the Newcastle-owned tug *Montrose* which arrived at Leith on 8 May and provided a duplicate service till early August. She was advertised by her charterer, Adam Gibb of Edinburgh as 'Lord Aberdour' but was not officially renamed, and was superior to the established vessels in possessing a deck saloon. Galloway was naturally upset, and showed it forcibly on 17 May when with the assistance of Alex Laing (owner of the tug *Blue Bonnet*) he obstructed passengers attempting to board 'Lord Aberdour' and physically assaulted her operator. He and Laing were charged the following day.

'Lord Aberdour' returned to Newcastle in August but her brief sojourn at Leith prompted MacGregor & Galloway to provide a proper excursion vessel for the Aberdour trade. Permission was obtained to name her *Lord Aberdour* and this landowner also gave a site near Hawkcraig Point, to the east of the quarries, for the construction of a wooden pier, suitable for landing at all states of the tide. The ship was built by Aitken & Mansel of Glasgow who produced a compact vessel with deck saloons fore and aft of her smooth-running oscillating engines. She was in commission for the 1866 season. The new pier followed soon afterwards though not specifically mentioned until 1870 when *Lord Aberdour* and *Pearl* were advertised as 'the only steamers that land passengers without small boats'. At this time all calls were at the 'New Pier' but from 1872 they reverted to the more convenient town, or stone, pier at high tide and the wooden pier became the low water landing.

A condition of the pier lease (which remained till 1918) was that it could not be used to land passengers on Sundays and on the partners' first Sunday run, on 2 August 1868, they stated 'N.B. This steamer lands her passengers with small boats. No intoxicated persons allowed on board.'

This trip incurred Lord Morton's wrath and rather than lose his goodwill the partners dropped Sunday sailing until 1870 when competition from rival owners forced MacGregor to run a seven-day service. A flory boat was provided for low water Sunday landings.

Portobello was by now emerging as a seaside resort, and in 1869 an Act was obtained by a private company to build a pier, 75ft from the north corner of Bath Street extending seawards for 1,250ft. Pier dues were set at the high price of 6d for passengers and 4d for promenaders. Thomas Bouch designed the elegant, cast-iron structure, which was laid out in the English manner with a saloon and entertainments on the pier. It was opened on 23 May 1871 and after the opening ceremony the official party embarked on the *Lord Aberdour* for a 1½ hour excursion along the coast to Inveresk and Prestonpans, followed by lunch in the pier saloon.

The first public sailing on the following Saturday was by the *Pearl* to Aberdour. Sailings were thereafter advertised by *Lord Aberdour* on Wednesdays and *Pearl* on Saturdays, but response was poor and the Wednesday sailing was abandoned by the end of June, and the Saturday one at the end of the season.

That was a year of experiment for the MacGregor fleet. *Lord Aberdour* on 23 August gave an unusual excursion from Leith at 5.30am, and Cockenzie 6am to St Andrews, returning at 7pm, while the 1866 *Blue Bonnet* (advertised as the 'New Blue Bonnet') made various excursions to Kirkcaldy, and to the Bass Rock and May Island. None were repeated, and from 1872–5

LEITH
AND
ABERDOUR.

On and after ~~TUESDAY~~ *Thursday* 1st JUNE the Saloon Steamer

"LORD ABERDOUR,"
OR OTHER STEAMER,

Sails daily as under (unless prevented by the weather or unforeseen circumstances, the Owners reserving the right of withdrawal at any time without notice)—

From LEITH (West Pier), at 7.30 and 11 a.m., 2 and 5 p.m.
From ABERDOUR, at 8.30 a.m., 12 Noon, 3 and 7 p.m.

ON SATURDAYS

From LEITH (West Pier), at 7.30 and 11 a.m., 2, 4, and 6 p.m.
From ABERDOUR, at 8.30 a.m., 12 Noon, 3, 5, and 7 p.m.

ON SUNDAYS

From LEITH (West Pier), at 12 Noon, 2.30 and 4.30 p.m.
From ABERDOUR, at 1, 3.30, and 7 p.m.

FARE - - NINEPENCE.

Passengers desirous of enjoying the Sail without Landing,

ONE FARE.

Works, Schools, or Large Parties carried at Reduced Rates.
Passengers are requested to take charge of their own Luggage.

MONTHLY AND SPECIAL TICKETS AT REDUCED RATES.
Apply to Collector on Board.

(Leith, *June* 1876.)

REID AND SON, PRINTERS, LEITH.

Advertisement of 1876 for Leith–Aberdour sailings

Lord Aberdour plied consistently on the Aberdour passage, assisted by *Pearl* on Sundays and other busy days. The other tugs were mostly disposed of during the fifties and sixties, the last to go being *Goliah* in 1871, *Blue Bonnet* in 1872, and the *Ruby* and *Pearl* in 1876.

John Galloway died on 25 April 1869, and his half share in the business passed to his widow, Margaret. On her death on 13 August, 1871 she was found to be bankrupt and the share was registered in the name of an Edinburgh chartered accountant. It passed to Galloway's son, Matthew Pearson in 1876, just before the last of the vessels was sold. The *Lord Aberdour* became solely MacGregor's property in April 1869.

The North Berwick Passage

The 'Geordie' tug owners watched MacGregor & Galloway's success with interest, and in 1866 Steedman, Hanson & Dykes placed their tug *Powerful* on a run every Thursday from the Shore at Leith (when tide allowed) and the West Pier, to North Berwick and the May Island, thus giving the first regular excursions to the outer firth. The sailings were not repeated in 1867 when *Powerful* was on charter to the Lighthouse Commissioners, but restarted the following season and the Thursday North Berwick Passage became a feature of the Forth sailings for the next twenty years. In 1870 a call at Portobello was added.

The *Powerful* also made Saturday afternoon excursions to Kirkcaldy in 1868/9, and in 1870 Dykes put his new iron tug *May* on Thursday and Saturday runs from the Shore at 12 noon and 3pm via the West Pier, to Burntisland and Inchcolm. Dykes, however, sold *May* that winter, but the North Berwick Passage continued with *Powerful* advertised by H. P. Hanson & Company.

Dykes returned in 1872 when *Powerful* was replaced by his new tugs the *William Scott* and *Integrity*. An Elie call with one hour ashore was substituted for the May Island call in 1873 but the run was not a financial success and in the following spring Dykes moved to Dundee. He had a new *May* built in 1875 and for the next few summers she appeared each Thursday at May Island and North Berwick on a cruise from Dundee. In 1879 she was back on the Forth sailing every Thursday from Leith in opposition to another tug. Again Dykes met with little success, and after trying unusual excursions to Dundee, Dunbar, and Prestonpans (Morrison's Haven) he withdrew from the east of Scotland shipping scene.

The Floating Shebeen

The tug *Garibaldi* was owned by a partnership of George Jamieson, T. Scott and Isabelle Stoker. In May 1867 Jamieson (who was master of the vessel) decided there was money to be made in the Sunday trade by exploiting the fact that shore licensing hours did not apply on board ship, and *Garibaldi* became a floating drinking palace. The excursions commenced on 4 July with two return services to Aberdour and were so well patronised that in 1868 a further crossing was added. Trips were also given on Saturdays, to the May Island with three hours ashore.

Garibaldi was the only Forth excursion ship to sink after a collision. It occurred on 14 August 1868. Fortunately she was empty, having just sailed from Newhaven stone pier. She rounded Leith West Pier as MacGregor's *Lord Aberdour* was leaving for Aberdour and the outgoing ship cut four feet off of her bow. *Garibaldi* sank immediately in the fairway, and remained on the bottom for several days. A public exchange of letters between Jamieson and John Galloway followed marking the start of ruthless competition between the two companies. *Storm King* was chartered to continue the Sunday season. *Garibaldi* returned in 1869 making regular trips to South Queensferry on Saturday afternoons in addition to her busy, boozy Sunday Aberdour runs. She was sunk for the second and final time on 17 June 1870 while towing off North Berwick. *Storm King* was again substituted by the partners, now G. Jamieson, J. Kerr, John and Thomas Stoker, but MacGregor's *Lord Aberdour* was now running on Sundays and was much preferred by the jovial travellers to Aberdour. Jamieson was forced to abandon that port and a service to both North and South Queensferry was substituted.

The 'Fiery Cross'

It seems possible that there were no Sunday sailings the next season but from 1872 occasional Sunday runs were made to Burntisland and Kirkcaldy by *Fiery Cross*, a newcomer to the fleet, and from 1873 the sole property of George Jamieson. She had no pretensions to beauty, or much in the way of passenger accommodation but was a colourful little vessel with a bright red hull, and absurdly tall white funnel with a deep black top and coloured band. She had the advantage of a good turn of speed and could outpace *Lord Aberdour*. These features, coupled with Jamieson's personality and imagination were destined to win her outstanding popularity with the ever increasing number of Forth excursionists.

In 1874 she took over the Thursday North Berwick run, circling the Bass Rock before her return up Firth. The Sunday ferry to Burntisland also became a regular feature and in 1875 Saturday cruises were reintroduced. Inchkeith, where fortifications were under construction, was a favourite destination, and passengers were allowed ashore to view the progress of the works.

With true crusading spirit *Fiery Cross* returned to the Sunday Aberdour run in 1876, and to the great delight of both Jamieson and his patrons proved the fastest of the several vessels on that station. Competition was brisk, and at Leith Jamieson berthed his ship upstream of the other ships, doing his best to lure passengers on board before they had a chance to see the saloon steamers lying further down the pier. Vigorous pier head touting developed and feelings ran high. On Sunday 27 August 1876, there was a fight on the pier which ended in Jamieson's arrest. The following morning, at Leith Police Court, he was fined 20s, and 'ordered to find caution for £3 to keep the peace for three months'. John Eunson, *Lord Aberdour*'s pier porter, appeared as prosecution witness and stated:

> that it was his duty to 'tout' for passengers. In doing so he became within a short distance of the gangway of the *Fiery Cross*. Jamieson came forward to him, and in a very excited manner, called him several filthy names and threatened to split his face. Eunson denied that he was in the habit of informing passengers that the accused's boat was 'an old rotten tug, not fit to carry passengers.'

Tugboat or not, *Fiery Cross* attracted passengers, and competition on the North Berwick run was beaten off by Jamieson extending the cruise to the May Island where he nosed his little ship into the rocks and gave his passengers the pleasure of two hours ashore. Jamieson held the monopoly of the run until 1884.

Fiery Cross, despite her lack of amenities, was providing the gregarious camaraderie which was desired, and by the end of the summer had a popular following who regarded her much as a family of today look on their car. She became known as much by her by-names, as her real one. To most Leithers she was either 'Auld Nonsuch' or 'Grannie's Washtub' (a name which aptly described her lines) while to her Sunday passengers she was best known as the 'Aiberdour Puddock' (dialect for frog—referring to the grasshopper motion from her engines) and to the more thirsty as the 'Floatin' Shebeen'. She was also referred to in at least one church sermon, as the 'fiery curse which desecrated the Sabbath on the waters of the Firth'.

From 1877 *Fiery Cross* became a full-time excursion ship giving runs to Elie and North Berwick in addition to her established Thursday and weekend sailings. In the following year the new Tay Bridge was attracting considerable attention at Dundee and cruises to it were added to the itinerary, with two hours ashore at Dundee and a cruise alongside the new bridge. By 1879 trippers were also being landed at Anstruther and St Andrews, and *Fiery Cross* was cruising up river to Stirling, also making several visits to the guard ship off Queensferry (HMS *Lord Warden*) where her passengers were allowed on board.

This success story continued in 1880 when Kirkcaldy became a regular port of call and *Fiery Cross* reached the peak of her popularity. Jamieson's fertile imagination was constantly devising new excursions. Special cruises were provided for Kirkcaldy market, Inverkeithing 'Lammas Fair', Alloa Fast Day, and even for a flower show at North Berwick. On Tuesday, 14 September, she sailed at 11am on a 'Shooting Excursion down the Forth, to the vicinity of the Bass Rock—parties will enjoy two or three hours shooting, and a boat will be lowered to pick up the birds'. At 2s it was a popular trip, and it was repeated late in the season for several years. Her small size and low overheads allowed her to enjoy a long season and in spring she was first boat out and continued late into the autumn still running to Aberdour on Sundays. On her last departure each year a large wooden cross soaked in pitch was erected at the stern and set alight as she sailed away into the gathering dusk. It made a splendid spectacle, leaving watchers on the shore in no doubt about which ship was passing by.

The Steam Packet Services

The established year-round passenger services to Stirling and to Anstruther, and the cargo service to Kincardine and Alloa continued for a surprisingly long time considering that Edinburgh and Stirling were connected by rail in 1849 and Anstruther (via the Burntisland ferry) in 1863.

The effect of the railway was most noticeable on the winter traffic and in 1853–4 the Alloa, Stirling & Kincardine Steamboat Company economised by terminating its service at Alloa. However, there were loud complaints from the Stirling merchants and in subsequent seasons the service ran as before all the way to Stirling. The *Prince of Wales* and the *Albert* continued as the regular steamers (except in June/July 1850 when the *Royal Victoria* replaced the latter) until 1858 when *Albert* was sent on an unusual voyage to Copenhagen and was lost at sea. She was replaced by the iron Clyde-built ship *Victoria* which then partnered the *Prince of Wales* for almost the next two decades.

During the 1860s the company's policy underwent a gradual transition with increased attention being paid to the tourist routes. In 1870, when most excursionists were automatically making their way to the West Pier at Leith, they abandoned Granton and brought the steamers into Leith, touting for traffic with the other craft. All pretension of operating a packet service was dropped, the sailings being advertised as excursions.

The company was wound up in May 1874 following the death of Alex Wingate, its principal proprietor. That summer the *Prince of Wales* was advertised in the name of the Stirling Steamboat Company and was probably owned by Walter Beveridge, a rather testy tugmaster at Alloa. She sailed from Granton but later started from Leith and called at Granton en route. At the end of the season she was sold to Clyde owners. *Victoria* was purchased by James Neill of Alloa and continued to sail on her old route, in the face of severe competition, until 29 August 1876. She went to the Mersey in January 1877.

The packet run between Anstruther and Leith included calls at Elie, Largo, Leven and Dysart. Traffic from these ports was light and only the Elie call (and occasionally Pittenweem) survived the summer of 1855. The exceptionally fine two-masted steamer *Forth* was built for the service in 1856, replacing the

23

Xantho which went to MacGregor & Galloway. She served the company, summer and winter, for the rest of its existence. As with the Stirling route, much of the trade was eventually lost to the railway and while the winter service was maintained, summer tourists latterly provided the main revenue and from 1871 'Cheap Day Trips to Anstruther' were advertised whenever the tide allowed. The service was discontinued after 18 May 1875, and *Forth* became a coal hulk at Granton harbour. The screw steamer *Cameo* maintained a goods service for the next two years and thereafter regular sailings to the East Neuk of Fife ceased.

The upriver cargo service by the elderly *Morning Star* and *Stirling Castle* was reduced to twice weekly sailings to Kincardine, and once to Alloa in 1856. *Morning Star* went to the breakers in 1856, but the old 'Stirling' remained in service until 1871 being assisted by the screw vessel *Alpheus* from 1864. A little vessel, *Carradale*, was also used after 1869 and in the middle seventies the *Corsair* was on the run. The regular service ceased with her sale in April 1878, but thereafter, until the early years of this century, the coasting steamers of A. F. Henry & MacGregor Limited made voyages to Alloa and Stirling whenever sufficient cargo was offered.

The Kidd Fleet

Donald MacGregor sold the *Lord Aberdour*, his principal shipping asset, in January 1874 to John Kidd, a Leith wine merchant. While Kidd's primary reason for entering the trade may have been to promote the sale of alcoholic spirits, he made a genuine attempt during his six years of ownership to improve the Forth excursions. He brought in Edward Newton as his partner but after a few months he was replaced by Anthony Watson who retained an interest until the late 1880s.

During 1874/5 the MacGregor tugs *Pearl* and possibly *Ruby*, assisted on Sundays and when required for charters. This continuity from the old management was due to the influence of John Galloway's son, M. P. Galloway, who had probably acted as unofficial manager since his father's death. This was a convenient arrangement, as in 1865 he had founded his own business in Leith as an engineer, ship chandler, and shipbuilder. It was a simple matter to handle the commercial side of the seasonal shipping trade through his office, and despite several subsequent changes in steamer ownership this practice continued until World War I. It was ratified in March 1876 when M. P. Galloway was officially appointed Manager for Kidd's steamer fleet.

Following the withdrawal of *Prince of Wales* from the Stirling run and the collapse of the Anstruther Steam Shipping Company in 1874–5, Kidd, in a bid for a monopoly of the Forth sailings, ordered two new steamers from Stockton-on-Tees. They were launched in March and April 1876 and named respectively *Lord Elgin* and *Lord Mar* (after the proprietors of upriver estates). They were the finest vessels built for service on the Forth to this time but surprisingly were not fitted with deck saloons, having instead a raised quarterdeck aft of the machinery giving a commodious main saloon, while a shade deck forward provided shelter for steerage passengers and adequate promenade facilities. At 160ft they were by far the largest vessels yet built for upriver traffic and were certified to carry 715 passengers. Compound diagonal machinery was fitted for smoothness and economy, a type of engine then in its infancy (and not used on the Clyde until 1889). It was the flaw in an otherwise perfect design. Though their speed was stated to be 12 knots, it is doubtful if more than 10 was ever achieved in normal service. Jamieson's *Fiery Cross* and even *Lord Aberdour* could pass them without difficulty.

On 1 April *Lord Elgin* opened the season on the Aberdour Passage and on 22 April the two ships commenced a daily service to Stirling, calling at Limekilns, Bo'ness, Kincardine, Alloa and (from 1878) Dunmore. One ship generally lay overnight at Alloa or Stirling to provide an early morning run to Leith, followed by a day cruise to Stirling. The second steamer was spare for the greater part of the day and gave the afternoon return service to Alloa or Stirling. Thus not only was an excursion service provided from Leith, but residents of Alloa and the other ports of call were offered day trips to Edinburgh. The ship designated as spare was, from early June, used for firth cruise work, and the results from the early cruises to North Berwick and round May Island, in competition with *Fiery Cross*, were so disappointing that Kidd's steamers never again called at North Berwick. Instead, a twice weekly service was given to Elie, with mid-week and Sunday services round the Bass Rock. A ferry service between Elie and North Berwick was given by *Pearl* on Saturday, 1 July, this being her last passenger sailing under Galloway's management.

Lord Mar was the victim of a serious fire on 28 August. While she was lying at the West Pier after a day cruise to Alloa, flames were noticed leaping from amidships at 8.30pm. Her moorings were loosened to allow her to drift into the channel to avoid damage to the pier while men from the tug *Gazelle* managed to release her boiler safety valves and connected a hose using the tug's donkey engine. It took the Leith fire brigade an hour and a half to arrive with their steam and manual engines, but by 11pm the fire was extinguished. After examination at the Shore her structure was found to be sound. She was back in service by Sunday, 8 October, when she took the Aberdour Passage sailings. It appears, however, that the repairs were not entirely satisfactory —possibly her hull was distorted—as *Lord Mar* was thereafter never used in open water and her future work was confined to the upriver and Aberdour services.

In reporting the fire, *The Scotsman* gave a full description of the interior layout, which gives an impression of the accommodation on these ships:

> . . . the fine spacious saloon is a complete wreck within, the only portion saved being the ladies' cabin which was protected by a strong partition. The mirrors and cabin furniture have been thoroughly destroyed . . . The refreshment bar on the starboard side of the ship is only distinguishable by the presence of broken decanters, the whole contents of the presses, cigars, liquors, and napery—having been destroyed. A considerable sum in paper money has also disappeared. The master, Page, has lost all his property placed in the bunk, and the engineer's apartment, . . . is a mass of embers. The space forward, to the galley, has been thoroughly consumed. Large quantities of ashes and other rubbish are scattered over the engines, and the steamer has now a strong list to port caused by the large quantity of water poured into her, . . . The engineer attributes the outbreak of fire to the overheating of the cement casing of the boilers, which caused the wooden surroundings to ignite. He states that the engines are little damaged . . .

The day after the fire James Neill abandoned the Stirling

service he was giving with *Victoria*, and chartered her to Galloway. She and *Lord Elgin* ran as partners for the remainder of the season, and as *Victoria* was sold during the following winter, her final service on the Forth was under Galloway's management.

With no competition upriver both the 'Lords' were employed on the Stirling run in 1877, apart from Saturday afternoon Bass Rock cruises and assisting on the Aberdour Passage on Sundays. An all-out effort was made to attract passengers. 'Tourists visiting Edinburgh are strongly recommended to travel to Alloa and Stirling . . . The scenery of the Firth of Forth is Magnificent and in many respects quite equal to the scenery of the Rhine.' Non-landing cruises were also featured, round the Alloa Inches on Sundays and on Wednesdays, 'sailing up the Forth on the South Side passing Granton, Inchmickery, Cramond Island, Barnbogle Castle, South Queensferry, Blackness Castle, etc., returning by the North Side passing Culross, Rosyth Castle, Inchcolm and Aberdour—a select band of music will accompany the steamer'. These did not prove successful, and by September had mostly been replaced by cruises to the Bass Rock.

There was sufficient river traffic for one ship and in 1878 *Lord Elgin* cruised round Bass on four days, to Elie and round May on two days, and weekly to Dundee 'sailing alongside and under the longest bridge in the world.' *Lord Mar* meanwhile maintained the Stirling service, assisting at Aberdour and cruising round the fortifications at Inchkeith on Sundays. During the Dundee holidays in late June both ships were based there for cruises to Perth, and round the Bell Rock. Receipts were disappointing from all the services, *Fiery Cross* skimming the cream of the traffic; and it was decided to dispose of *Lord Mar*. She was sold on 29 March 1879 and steamed out to Pernambuco (now Recife) in Brazil where she was resold for £6,200. It was a remarkable voyage for a steamer with such an unsatisfactory history but confirmation of her safe arrival was received by the Leith Customs Officer on 4 July.

Galloway attempted in 1879 to cover the needs of the entire area with *Lord Elgin*. The Stirling run was only given on three or four days every other week, when the tide allowed a departure from Leith between 10 and 11.30am. Otherwise she cruised much as before, and was again based at Dundee at the end of June. Again results were disappointing, and in 1880 a second attempt was made to induce Stirling traffic. The only firth sails were Saturday afternoon cruises round the Bass.

John Kidd died on 29 April 1880 and at the end of that season his executors agreed to dispose of the unfortunate *Lord Elgin*. She was sold in May 1881 for £5,000 to the Bournemouth & Swanage Steam Packet Company, proving a successful steamer for them. In 1909 her owners were taken over by the Southampton & Isle of Wight Company, and in 1914 after the outbreak of hostilities, *Lord Elgin* was transferred to Southampton to work the ferry service to Cowes. After the war, considered too old and slow for passenger work, she was converted to a cargo carrier, reappearing in June 1921, with an upright funnel, a 3-ton derrick, and with all the seating removed from the main deck. She then ran from Southampton to Cowes five days per week, summer and winter, and continued to do so for the next thirty-two years, being finally laid up in 1953, and broken up two years later.

At the time of her withdrawal, she was the oldest paddle steamer in Great Britain, having given forty-five years' service on excursions, followed by thirty-two years all-year-round cargo work—a total of seventy-seven years. Such service has been equalled by very few steamships, and speaks volumes for the craftsmanship which went into her construction, and the high standards specified by John Kidd and M. P. Galloway.

To operate *Lord Aberdour* the executors, Thomas Aitken, David Kidd, Mrs Annie Kidd, Anthony Watson, and M. P. Galloway formed a partnership titled the Forth River Steam Shipping Company and she continued, as for the previous fifteen seasons, on the Leith to Aberdour Passage run.

To complete the story of the pleasure excursions of the 1870s mention must be made of Henry Burrell of Grangemouth, who in 1878 brought his tug *Livingstone* to Leith on Saturdays, and gave cruises to Kirkcaldy, with the occasional variation of a sail to South Queensferry. He did not repeat these in other summers but in the 1880s, *Livingstone*, under different ownership, reappeared at Leith.

Chapter III

The Excursion Heyday
1881–1898

A Boom Year

In the spring of 1881 *Fiery Cross* and *Lord Aberdour* were the
only excursion vessels remaining on the Forth, but they did not
long enjoy a monopoly. The excursion traffic increased until
seven steamers were plying for trade.

Interest centred on *Carrick Castle*, an eleven-year-old Clyde
steamer which had been purchased by the Glasgow partnership
of Matthew & Mathieson and brought round to the east coast.
Her first cruises from Leith were on the Queen's birthday, 19
May, when she sailed twice to the Bass Rock and once in the
evening to Aberdour.

Next day *The Scotsman* commented: 'In this fast mail boat,
Elie could be reached in an hour, and Dundee in little over
three.' The Forth had never seen a ship so large and so fast, and
it was her speed which drew in the crowds. Within a few weeks
her advertisements were subtitled 'The Swiftest on the East
Coast'. She was of smart appearance though her accommodation
was old fashioned with low-ceilinged, ill-lit saloons and only a
diminutive deckhouse. Her powerful single diagonal engine
produced a strong surging motion which could be unpleasant on
a long journey. Her high speed made long excursions practical
and every Thursday she sailed round the Bass, May and Bell.
Cruises to Dundee were also frequent, and occasional trips were
made down the Haddington coast as far as St Abb's Head.
Upriver cruises were made to Alloa, where she was based during
the local fair holidays. On Edinburgh holidays she usually ran
to Aberdour.

Matthew Brydie, a legal writer in Alloa, was persuaded to restart the daily (Monday–Saturday) Stirling service with which his predecessors in office had been closely associated through the Alloa & Stirling Steamboat Company. The tug *Transit* was chartered for this duty and ran throughout the summer. In August she was joined by Walter Beveridge's *Blue Bonnet* and for a few weeks the two tugs had a daily race up the river. On certain days *Blue Bonnet* started from Alloa, providing a Stirling connection for *Carrick Castle*'s cruise from Leith.

The appearance of *Carrick Castle* immediately affected George Jamieson's trade and the only long cruises now given by *Fiery Cross* were her established Thursday sailings to North Berwick and the May Island. On other days she provided short excursions to Inchkeith, Inchcolm, Queensferry and Aberdour. Her departures from Leith were much more frequent than in the past and by aggressive 'touting' a reasonable trade was attracted.

Henderson & McKean of Leith purchased *Livingstone* for towing work but she gave cruises each weekend to Inchkeith or Aberdour. In August *Livingstone* brought the Duke of Edinburgh ashore to open the Edinburgh Dock, and for the rest of the season she was advertised as 'under Royal patronage'. The one-time Galloway vessel *Pearl* also briefly reappeared on passenger work and during the Edinburgh holidays gave a service to Kirkcaldy.

It was a poor season for the newly formed Forth River Steam Shipping Company as the frequent departure of rival steamers from Leith depleted the receipts from their Aberdour Passage. Their manager, M. P. Galloway, was a summer resident at Aberdour and a daily commuter to Leith on his own steamer. On 17 May 1880 he had acquired a fue at Hawkcraig, at the entrance to the low water pier, and had a large family house built nearby. He announced on 19 June that *Lord Aberdour* would cease to ply on Sundays 'in deference to the wishes of the visitors and others at Aberdour'. Jamieson quickly retaliated by doubling his service, chartering the Stirling vessel *Transit* to assist *Fiery Cross* in maintaining an hourly Sunday service to Aberdour.

A New Saloon Fleet

Agreement was reached between the rival Alloa owners in the autumn of 1881, Beveridge withdrawing *Blue Bonnet* from passen-

30

ger work and co-operating with Brydie in maintaining the service. *Transit* was returned to her owners at the end of the season and on 26 October Brydie purchased the Loch Lomond saloon steamer *Princess of Wales* and during the winter brought her to Alloa via the Clyde and the Caledonian Canal. Built alongside *Lord Aberdour* in 1866, she had an identical hull and machinery but her saloons were both larger and more comfortable. Aft of the paddles her deck was wider than the hull, adding to her spaciousness, and with her funnel placed forward of the paddles her profile was better balanced than that of her contemporary.

She opened the Stirling service in the spring of 1882, but had a short season, being laid up after her run on Saturday, 19 August. Construction of the swing bridge above Alloa had started in April, and though the channel was supposed to be kept clear for shipping, the contractors barely fulfilled this obligation. Staging blocked the entire river, except for 57ft at the site of the northern of the two opening spans and even this was regularly closed as piling work progressed. Shipping frequently was held up for one to two hours and the strong tide made holding a ship as large as *Princess of Wales* impractical.

After a lapse of one week George Jamieson took over this service, Thursdays and Sundays excepted, and maintained it till August 1883. *Fiery Cross* was small enough to negotiate the bridge opening, though the long delays waiting for the river to be cleared caused very late running. Letters sent to the contractors by Jamieson's solicitors and Stirling Town Council produced no improvement.

Princess of Wales was sold in May 1883 to John Cran, a Leith engineer, and from 1 August Walter Beveridge chartered her. She commenced running between Leith and Stirling the following day. Approaching the bridge she was caught by a current which threw her against the north-east pillar of the northern span. The span was completely demolished, and *Princess of Wales* withdrawn for repairs for twelve days. She did not attempt the Stirling service again that summer, terminating her run at Alloa.

By the following spring, conditions at the bridge had improved, so Beveridge purchased the ship and restarted the sailings. Though there was competition as far as Alloa only, he was prepared to sail further and his advertisement stated that:

31

Owing to other steamers not being able to pass through the new Forth Bridge at Alloa, passengers desirous of seeing the beautiful windings of the Forth between Alloa and Stirling, can only do so by travelling with the *Princess of Wales*.

The Forth River Steam Shipping Company had to act quickly if it were to survive, and in 1882 Galloway doubled the frequency of the weekday Aberdour Service by chartering *Livingstone*. (On Sundays Jamieson chartered her for the same purpose). This experiment proved a great success 'having induced a larger number of families to engage summer houses'. The transfer of *Fiery Cross* to the Stirling route also helped the company and in the autumn the partners agreed to maintain a two-ship service.

The Wallace brothers, Andrew, an Edinburgh solicitor, and Dr John, a doctor of medicine in Liverpool, joined the partnership to finance a new steamer and the order was placed with S. & H. Morton for an enlarged and faster version of *Lord Aberdour*. Named *Lord Morton*, she ran trials on the Gullane measured mile on 23 April 1883, attaining over 13 knots. She also did steaming trials upriver to Bo'ness, and made a trial call at Aberdour. Her machinery was of the straightforward single diagonal design with steam supplied from a double-ended boiler, requiring two funnels forward of the paddles. Due to excess weight forward *Lord Morton* steamed noticeably down by the head. She entered service with a Saturday cruise to Alloa, and then settled down as the Aberdour Passage steamer, with *Lord Aberdour* as consort. On her commissioning the fare was reduced from 9d to 6d, a rate which was retained until World War I, even when sailings were made via Queensferry.

From 6 to 10 August while *Princess of Wales* was under repair, *Lord Morton* operated successful day excursions to Alloa with connecting coach tours to beauty spots such as Dollar, Alva, Rumbling Bridge, and the ancient burgh of Culross. Robert Croall of the well known coaching family agreed to join the partnership. With his backing an order was placed with S. & H. Morton for another new ship.

The design was modelled on that of *Lord Morton* but to facilitate upriver navigation she was ten feet shorter, and the fore cabin was omitted to give better trim. She was a most successful steamer, free from the defects of her predecessor, and with furnishings tastefully designed to attract the better class tourist:

> The fittings generally are of the best material, the upper saloon has been handsomely cushioned in olive green velvet, the break-fast and dining saloon in crimson velvet, and the forecabin in haircloth. Ventilation has been carefully attended to, and lava-tories are fitted on each side of the deck saloon. The vessel has accommodation for between 700 and 800 passengers.

Named *Stirling Castle*, she sailed on 29 March 1884 on a proving trip, to ensure that she could navigate the Alloa railway bridge where temporary staging still blocked all but 57ft of the river. Steaming round the west side of the Alloa Inch she allowed herself the minimum time to line up to pass the bridge-works. As she approached she slowed to half speed, and was caught by a side current which swept her into the north-east pier of the structure. Ship and bridge were considerably damaged and *Stirling Castle* returned to Leith for repairs, reappearing for her trial trip on Tuesday 22 April when she steamed to Alloa and back at just under 14 knots.

The bridge contractors meanwhile had removed some of the staging, clearing the full 60ft span for shipping, and fitted fen-ders round the bridge piers. They then served notice on S. & H. Morton for damages caused by careless navigation. With the river clear, Walter Beveridge restarted his Stirling service but Galloway decided that *Stirling Castle*'s run would terminate at Alloa until the court case had been settled.

The service started on 1 May calling at Bo'ness and Kincar-dine, and the connecting coach tours commenced four days later. On the first, which was fairly typical, passengers sailed to Alloa and then coached to Dollar, rejoining the steamer at Kincardine for their return journey. Inclusive fares for the trips were from 4s to 4s 6d. On most days a second coach tour was advertised to Stirling, but it did not prove popular, passengers preferring the direct Stirling boat. Galloway slanted his advertisement to imply that the ship sailed to Stirling. His rival's publicity made it clear that it did not!

The case against S. & H. Morton was dismissed in May 1885 and the bridge contractors were severely censured for interfering with the river navigation in contravention of the Alloa Railway Act. The bridge had upset the flow of the flood tide, causing strong cross eddies. The only way for a ship to hold her course was to maintain full speed, and any delay at the bridge would be highly dangerous. *Stirling Castle* and *Lord Aberdour* (probably at the expense of the Caledonian Railway) were fitted with hinged masts and telescopic funnels to allow them to pass under the closed bridge. Thus equipped *Stirling Castle* proudly made her debut at Stirling Shore on 20 May 1885.

As noted, *Fiery Cross* was on the Stirling run in 1883 when construction of the cantilever railway bridge at Queensferry commenced. Jamieson soon found his little ship carrying increasing numbers of tourists, curious to see how this bridge work was progressing. By midsummer he was giving special 'bridge cruises' landing at South Queensferry, and in 1884 he dropped all other sailings except the Thursday May Island run. *Fiery Cross* then gave a ferry service to South Queensferry six days a week. The Forth River Steam Shipping Company also started bridge cruises in 1884 operating *Stirling Castle* to North Queensferry and *Lord Aberdour* to South Queensferry on Sundays.

Throughout this period *Carrick Castle* continued to reign supreme. In 1882 she had invaded the Sunday Aberdour station, depriving Jamieson of much of his trade, with the result that he did not charter an extra vessel the following year and withdrew from the station altogether in 1884. Her cruises eventually covered all the major ports and resorts. This even included Perth, to which she sailed via Dundee on at least two occasions. She also introduced regular evening cruises in 1883, usually sailing to the Forth Bridge works.

Famous Names Vanish

Carrick Castle was sold to south of England owners and left the Forth on 2 May 1885. On the previous day Walter Beveridge had died suddenly at Alloa. His sons, knowing that Galloway would run to Stirling that summer, took *Princess of Wales* to Dundee and there she became a well-known pleasure steamer over the next quarter of a century.

The withdrawal of these vessels left the Forth River Steam Shipping Company in a very strong position and Sunday sailings to Aberdour were restarted. In mid July the new much publicised service to Stirling was temporarily reduced to three days a fortnight, freeing *Stirling Castle* for an experimental cruise programme, involving day and afternoon trips via Portobello to Elie, Anstruther, May Island, and occasionally North Berwick, with non-landing cruises to the Bass Rock, Fidra and Aberlady Bay. Forth Bridge and evening cruises were also given whenever ships could be spared. Reviewing the position in the autumn the partners were delighted with the results.

Thus encouraged, an order for an additional steamer was placed with Scott's of Kinghorn. Agreement was reached with Queensferry Town Council to build an all-tide landing, seaward from the Town Harbour. At this stage the proprietors were registered as:

Thomas Aitken	4/64	Annie Maria Merse or	
Robert Croall	4/64	Kidd	10/64
Matthew P. Galloway	12/64	Andrew Wallace	12/64
David Kidd	5/64	Dr. John Wallace	12/64
		Anthony Watson	5/64

George Jamieson also had a successful season in 1885 and though *Fiery Cross*'s sailings still concentrated on Queensferry, she fitted in two extra Forth cruises most weeks—to Elie, sometimes via North Berwick, and she recaptured some of her former glory. It was, however, the last season when she counted as a major force. Jamieson, with no family following in the business, allowed it to run down.

In 1886, after the opening of Galloway's new pier, Jamieson cancelled his bridge cruises and also had to face opposition for the Thursday traffic to North Berwick and May Island. In 1887 he diverted this cruise to Dunbar or round the Bass. *Fiery Cross*'s only other sailings were on Saturdays to Inchkeith and Kirkcaldy. The ship appeared rarely, if at all, in 1888, but returned the following year on an unusual ferry service between Leith and Inchkeith. She was present at the opening of the Forth Bridge in March 1890 and made her last public cruise one week later, on 12 April 1890, appropriately to the bridge. Jamieson died in September 1893, and his famous little ship was broken up five years later after working as a tug at Leith, and latterly Grangemouth.

The Galloway Saloon Steam Packet Company

On 9 April 1886 the Forth River Steam Company Shipping was dissolved and re-registered as The Galloway Saloon Steam Packet Company. Thomas Aitken, David Kidd and Andrew Wallace were directors, with the first named acting as chairman; M. P. Galloway became managing owner. Capital of £32,000 was issued in £10 shares, but soon proved insufficient and was increased by £12,000 (of which £8,450 was paid up) on 17 November. R. Croall became the major shareholder by buying out Mrs Kidd. All shares were issued on a pro-rata basis to the F.R.S.S. holdings and in November 1887 the holdings were:

T. Aitken	445	D. Kidd	250	Dr. J. Wallace	809
R. Croall	944	A. Wallace	809	A. Watson	250
M. P. Galloway	809				

Speaking at the annual general meeting in November 1886, Thomas Aitken stated that the lack of proper low water landing stages presented the greatest obstacle to the operation of the excursion trade, and the company's policy must be to give first priority to their provision. The only places where vessels could call regardless of tide were Leith, Portobello, Kirkcaldy, Aberdour (where the company already owned the low water pier) and Alloa. Kincardine could be reached at most times, but elsewhere calls were either severely restricted or flory boats were in frequent use. The new company had already concluded negotiations at South Queensferry and there a long pier was opened on 4 June 1886, by a call from *Stirling Castle*. The pier allowed the company to cater adequately for the tourists crowding to view the railway bridge.

At North Berwick, a notoriously difficult call, negotiations for a pier site on the Platock Rocks opened in April 1886. The contract was let on 9 February 1887 and it was hoped to have the pier in service that summer. However, the iron was late, then sand was discovered where rock was expected. The pier was opened in 1888. *Stirling Castle* made the first call on 25 May and took the Provost and councillors on a luncheon cruise to Elie.

The company had plans to give Largo (a delightful village with beautiful sands) a ferry service on the lines of the Aberdour

Passage. A survey for a pier was made in September 1886, but after objections from the local landowner the Board of Trade refused the foreshore lease and the plan had to be shelved. It was resurrected in 1889 when the company decided to provide a moving gangway for landings by flory boat. Again the local land-owner objected and the Board of Trade refused permission. The gangway, a long eight-wheeled structure, had been constructed and was placed on Lundin Beach, a mile east of the village. A pier at this site was considered but again local opposition defeated the project.

By contrast, at Elie the company easily obtained approval for a landing stage on the rocks outside the harbour. It was completed and brought into use in 1889 but at low water that summer the steamers damaged their paddles on projecting rocks. This difficulty was overcome by fitting an extra row of piling the following winter.

A Sunday service being operated to Kirkcaldy roused considerable local opposition and early in 1888 an injunction was filed against the company prohibiting Sunday calls. Andrew Wallace won the case, enabling the sailings to be resumed in August 1888.

Charlestown was added to the list of river calls on 13 August 1889, by the North British Railway granting a lease of the old steamboat berth on the outside wall of the harbour. This jetty was rebuilt for the 1890 season.

Portobello was a valuable call. It collected traffic not only from the thriving resort itself, but also from the east Edinburgh and Musselburgh area. The pier was badly damaged by one of the steamers in June 1887 and closed for ten days while repairs were made. Damages were settled in November 1888 when the pier company received £837 19s 1d. In the eighteen years of its existence the pier company had never declared a dividend and the accident broke it financially. In 1889 the G.S.S.P. provided a subsidy of £200, and the company continued to keep the pier open. In June 1891 the Steam Packet Company purchased the pier outright for £1,500.

While the various piers were being acquired or rebuilt the company gave its steamers a new look. The prosaic black hulls and black-topped yellow funnels gave way in 1886 to hulls of violet-grey, topped by varnished deck cabins, sponson houses in a lighter tone of violet, paddleboxes in brilliant white, and funnels in navy yellow. Smart new officers' uniforms with a gold braid letter 'G' on the yachting cap completed the impression of a passenger yacht.

The general-purpose vessel, ordered during the last months of the partnership, *Edinburgh Castle*, ran her trials on 8 May 1886. For the first time in a Forth ship the deck saloons extended to the full width of the hull, giving increased internal comfort and a spacious top deck, 95ft long and 20ft broad. In internal layout she was similar to her immediate predecessors. The 70ft long dining saloon was upholstered in crimson velvet. Cooking equipment was heated by steam from the main boiler, and a similar arrangement kept the dishes warm in the saloon bars. Electric lighting was fitted, for the first time on a Forth ship, while the machinery was of the well-tried single diagonal type, with steam supplied at 60lb pressure by a haystack boiler. The single funnel was telescopic, and the mast hinged down. On trial a speed of 15 knots was maintained between the west point of Inchkeith and the new Oxcar light, a recognised distance of 5 miles.

Edinburgh Castle was to prove one of the Forth's most popular and reliable steamers. During her first season she showed herself too lively for comfort in the short steep seas encountered at the mouth of the firth and most of her subsequent career was spent on more sheltered services.

On 9 April 1887 Scott launched *Tantallon Castle*, the new flagship of the company. She ran trials on 28 May when a speed of 15 knots was recorded over the measured mile at Gullane:

> The main saloon on deck, with the ladies saloon adjoining are upholstered in old gold plush, and the former room is beautifully furnished in carved teak wood. Immediately below . . . is the well ventilated dining saloon laid in crimson cloth, with tables in the centre, and seated for nearly 100 persons. Electric light is supplied by an iron-clad dynamo and Archer engine. 30 incandescent lights, of 20 candlepower each, illuminate the ship, and a bridge lamp is fitted to allow of the passengers landing with safety, on returning from the evening cruises.

A single-cylinder diagonal engine was fed with steam from a haystack boiler which had the unusual feature of two blow-off pipes, one on each side of the funnel.

For the 1887 season all the vessels were fitted with flying bridges (introduced the previous summer on *Edinburgh Castle*) and *Lord Morton* and *Stirling Castle* were also equipped with electric lighting for use on evening cruises. The latter received the installation from the *Edinburgh Castle* as her roster did not now involve running after dark.

The fleet veteran, *Lord Aberdour*, was well past her best. A company minute of March 1887 states that her boiler had been repaired 'and was expected to be all right this season'! It was not, and a year later was removed for repairs costing over £400. Her accommodation, also, did not match the high standard introduced in the newer ships and at the annual general meeting in 1888 Andrew Wallace complained of her being in service at all.

Services were developed to exploit the available ships and piers. The Stirling route, with its ramifications of connecting coach tours, got a daily service (Sundays excepted) from 1886, this being maintained by *Stirling Castle*. The two 'Lords' (assisted on Sundays by the 'Stirling') catered for the needs of Aberdour and Queensferry, while *Edinburgh Castle* took up the sailings on the open Firth. These were based on a Largo passage with morning and evening runs for summer commuters, and a daily sailing at 10am which returned at 3pm. On weekdays this extended into a cruise round the Bass Rock (Mondays and Wednesdays), to the Bell Rock (Tuesdays), May Island (Thursdays), and to St Abb's Head on Fridays. By July all these cruises were calling additionally at Elie and on Wednesdays the evening service was extended to a cruise, either to Anstruther or round the Bass Rock.

There were no immediate alterations following delivery of *Tantallon Castle*. She took over the Elie services from the 'Edinburgh' which was transferred to the Stirling run while the 'Stirling' joined *Lord Morton* on the Aberdour and Queensferry runs. *Lord Aberdour* was relegated to the role of spare steamer, but deputised frequently for *Stirling Castle* which made many extra runs to Queensferry. The 'Tantallon' gave several special long cruises with destinations as far afield as Dundee, and the Farne Islands. On these days the 'Stirling' covered the Elie sailings.

After only a week in service *Tantallon Castle* was coasting towards the eastern berth at Portobello with the mooring ropes secured, when the slide valve on her reversing engine seized. Unable to go astern to take her way off, she drifted up the pier with the flood tide pushing her steadily nearer, until her sponson eventually went underneath the pier deck and hit the cast-iron supporting columns. The ship finished up aground on the sands with the pier on top of her. Only twenty minutes later she floated off with the tide and steamed out astern, and the other side of the pier broke away, 140ft of it collapsing into the water.

The pier was closed for ten days while a temporary wooden structure was erected to join the remaining portions. Permanent repairs were made the following winter. *Tantallon Castle* had her bridge rails and davits carried away but was back in service within a week.

The sailing programme for 1888 was more intensive, embracing the new pier at North Berwick and including cruises from the Firth resorts to the Forth Bridge. The 'Tantallon' and 'Stirling' were both employed on cruise work; the 'Tantallon' frequently sailing direct from Leith to Elie where she collected the cruise passengers brought by the smaller ship from Portobello and North Berwick. The 'Stirling' combined this feeder service with a comprehensive programme of bridge cruises, which included minor or difficult calls like Buckhaven and Dunbar. The 'Lords' were left to cope with the Aberdour and Queensferry traffic, which heavily taxed their capacity and during the following summer Henderson & McKean's tug *Gladstone* was chartered. The 1889 season proved a record one, the fleet having reached its maximum of six ships and carrying over 380,000 passengers.

Relations between the Steam Packet Company and the NBR were cool. On 1 July 1889 the railway company sent a strong letter to the GSSP complaining of interference with its traffic. Private negotiations commenced immediately between the NBR and all the GSSP Co shareholders except the Wallace brothers. On 25 July, Messrs Aitken, Croall, Galloway, Kidd and Watson agreed to sell 2,698 of their shares back to the company. Andrew Wallace (who also represented his brother in Liverpool) opposed the motion. The shares were snapped up for the NBR by nominees acting on behalf of its marine subsidiary, the North British Steam Packet Company. The shares were officially transferred on 13 December, after an acrimonious general meeting at which Andrew Wallace left his colleagues in no doubt about what he thought of their action.

The NBR thus acquired a 62½ per cent holding in the Galloway business. The board was reconstituted with strong NBR representation, but with A. Wallace still a member, Thomas Aitken as chairman and M. P. Galloway as manager. There was no outward sign of change, and despite the railway interest the Galloway Saloon Steam Packet Company remained firmly managed from Leith.

Palmy Summers

Throughout most of the 1890s the Galloway Saloon Steam Packet Co enjoyed a halcyon period which represented the heyday of pleasure sailing on the Forth. Every April the 'Leith Yachts' reappeared in immaculate condition. Continued attention to maintenance ensured a smart turnout all season and the public was offered a magnificent selection of sailings and tours at remarkably low prices, with excellent catering and timekeeping.

In the 1890 season the steamers came out in March for the opening of the Forth Bridge. *Thane of Fife* was chartered from the NBR for the Edinburgh holiday on 22 May, and a ferry was also chartered from 7 June to 6 September. In June the vessel probably was *Thane of Fife* but by late July the much larger *John Stirling* was in use to provide ample capacity for the Aberdour traffic.

The use of ferries was a temporary measure for they were either too slow or drew too much water. Tenders were therefore requested for a new ship. Only three were received, and since the lowest represented a 50 per cent increase over the cost of *Tantallon Castle* the project was dropped.

The NBR offered its newly reboilered eighteen-year-old Clyde steamer *Gareloch* at a price of £4,000. Of raised quarterdeck design, she was not up to the standard of the newer ships, but with no better alternative available the board was thankful to accept her.

She entered service in July 1891 after alterations by Menzies & Company enabled her to obtain a class 3 BOT certificate. She was renamed *Wemyss Castle* and, repainted in the Galloway colours, looked a smart vessel. Her typical Clyde profile gave an elegance which the Forth-built ships lacked and she was faster than her associates on the Aberdour/Queensferry runs and of greater carrrying capacity, all features which compensated in fair measure for her lack of deck saloons.

The Aberdour and Queensferry services were always the 'bread and butter' runs of the company, being the first to start in spring and the last to finish in autumn. By the 1890s three ships were used on these services, each with its distinctive schedule. *Lord Morton* worked triangularly, sailing direct to Aberdour in the mornings and returning via Queensferry. In the afternoons her route was reversed, giving day visitors to Aberdour a direct sailing while those out for the cruise enjoyed a view of the Forth Bridge. In 1891 the two other ships—*Wemyss Castle* and *Lord Aberdour*—worked direct, one to Queensferry and the other to Aberdour but as the novelty of the Forth Bridge wore off and the number of passengers actually landing at Queensferry declined, all the rosters became triangular. Evening cruises were run frequently to the bridge from Portobello and Aberdour as well as from Leith and were a speciality of the electrically lit *Lord Morton* and *Stirling Castle*.

Edinburgh Castle was firmly attached to the Stirling route, running five or six days a week at times which suited the tidal flow. She achieved some very fast runs and with five intermediate calls was allowed only three hours for the 45 mile trip. Whenever possible she was based at Leith, but on one day each fortnight she made three single journeys, followed by three or four days of excursion work from Stirling. On these she had a long idle spell at Leith in the middle of the day, which she sometimes filled in with a '12 o'clock cruise' round Inchkeith and upriver as far as Blackness. On Saturdays she often gave additional runs to Queensferry, and an upriver cruise to Alloa, while on Sundays she maintained a morning and evening Kirkcaldy service, with an upriver trip to Alloa or Grangemouth.

The main Firth cruise programme was taken by the *Tantallon Castle* and on weekdays consisted of a day cruise calling at Elie and North Berwick. The destination was most frequently either the Bell or Bass Rocks, or May Island. At suitable tides this cruise started from Alloa and picked up passengers at the river towns before leaving Leith. Evening cruises round the Bass Rock, calling at either Kirkcaldy or Portobello, were featured on most Fridays. On Saturdays a double run was given to Elie, with an afternoon cruise round the Bass, while Sunday was the day for the special long cruises, St Andrews being one of the most popular destinations, with Dundee and Berwick-on-Tweed featured from time to time.

As secondary Firth cruise ship, *Stirling Castle* made a number of excursions from the resorts to Queensferry, as well as a variety of day and afternoon cruises. She was the ship most usually seen at Kirkcaldy, Buckhaven, Methil (for Leven) and Largo (where a coach tour ran to Falkland). Liner tendering, charter, and relief work was all allocated to her, and on Saturdays she gave assistance with the Queensferry traffic, and occasional sailings to or from Grangemouth. On Sundays her regular sailing combined a double run to Methil with a cruise round the Bass Rock.

An attempt was made in the late eighties to develop commuting traffic from Largo (1886) and Elie (from 1887). This was expanded in 1889 by the provision of separate vessels for each resort but these services did not prove profitable, Largo being dropped after 1889 and the Elie runs restricted to Mondays, Wednesdays and Fridays in 1891. Despite a petition from the Elie residents the service was abandoned at the end of that season.

The other services continued each year with only minor changes and improvements. Calls at Kirkcaldy, Methil and Largo increased yearly and an innovation in 1896 was evening cruises to Pettycur, where the last call by a steamer had been made over fifty years earlier. The Firth cruise ship also stopped there every Monday and Friday that season in place of the call at Portobello. Circle tickets were introduced in 1897 by steamer to Queensferry or Stirling, returning by train. Through booking facilities were also arranged from most Fife stations, joining the cruise steamer at Elie. Outwardly there was every sign of prosperity and the public had come to accept the sailings as part of the natural summer scene on the Forth.

At Board level the position did not look so rosy as there had been heavy expenditure throughout the decade and the company never realised the profits its promoters had hoped for. From 1896 there was no dividend, and in preceding years it had barely averaged 5 per cent.

The most consistent drain had been the continual repairs required at Portobello pier, which was in poor condition when acquired in 1891. This was a remarkable structure, unique in Scottish resorts in that it provided tearoom, entertainment, fishing

43

and promenade facilities in the English manner, with steamer calls almost of secondary consequence. A new bandstand was provided by the SP Company, only to be twisted and battered in a storm on 20 September 1891 (the autumn holiday), which swept the tearoom into the sea and so damaged the pier that it was not reopened until May 1893, twenty months later. When reopened, bar, tearoom and ballroom were all provided, but the Magistrates declined to grant a licence for such an immoral practice as dancing and it had to stop! They were only too happy to levy rates, however, and the bill for £250 shocked the company.

By the winter of 1894–5 more repairs were needed and long iron girders were fitted on each side to hold the piles together. A dancing licence was finally obtained in 1896 but in July a minor accident involving the *Tantallon Castle* caused further speculation about safety and the Board of Trade prohibited all pier entertainment. The pier was closed from Friday to Monday each week while emergency strengthening work was carried out. A survey the following spring showed that it was still unsafe. Menzies of Leith was given a contract worth £1,127 17s 1d for repairs, but grossly exceeded this figure after a diving examination proved that many of the piles were almost completely rusted away at their bases and required reinforcing by steel bands. In 1897, for the first time since its purchase, Portobello pier was considered fully safe.

The north-east gale on the autumn holiday of 1891 also caught four of the ships lying completely unprotected at the West Pier, Leith. All suffered considerable damage from grinding against the pier. The fore-saloon and side house of *Edinburgh Castle* were smashed in and she also sustained hull damage; *Stirling Castle* had stanchions, a paddlebox and a lifeboat stove in. On *Lord Morton* there was severe damage to the entire sponson, paddlebox and side houses, which all had to be replaced. *Wemyss Castle* escaped lightly with her main rail, bulwark and several stanchions smashed. During the next five years the newest ships all required major unbudgeted expenditure. Next was *Stirling Castle*, in which the main crankshaft was replaced after a crack was discovered on 4 August 1893.

Experience with *Tantallon Castle* showed that her steaming properties left much to be desired. The boiler produced very wet steam and after two or three seasons a much taller funnel was fitted to increase the draught. Even so, she required reboilering after only seven seasons and a replacement boiler was recommended in July 1894. It was fitted by Ramage & Ferguson the following spring when to improve her trim the ship was lengthened by 13ft, the extra portion being inserted behind the engine room. The alterations, costing £1,660, greatly enhanced her appearance but wet steam remained a problem, finally being cured by S. & H. Morton in May 1897 with the fitting of an auxiliary condenser which produced 3in additional vacuum, and increased the engine revolutions by 5 per cent.

Edinburgh Castle was reported as giving boiler trouble in May 1896, and was reboilered the following winter by Gourley Bros & Company of Dundee. This installation proved faulty and in September 1897 she was handed over to Ramage & Ferguson, Gourley Bros accepting liability for repairs.

In contrast to the heavy repairs required on the prestige ships, the Aberdour fleet gave little trouble; with the predictable exception of *Lord Aberdour*. Several of her hull plates were condemned in the spring of 1893, and had to be doubled from the inside. This process required removal of the engine, which proved an expensive operation. Four years later her boiler was condemned, but was passed after a patch-up repair by John Cran & Sons which gave her two more years of service.

By the middle of the decade it was Galloway's opinion that an adequate service could be provided using only five steamers. In May 1896 a Captain Wiggins and some Russian gentlemen expressed interest in *Wemyss Castle* and the board agreed to sell on almost any terms. Unfortunately, Captain Wiggins purchased the one-year-old Clyde steamer *Glenmore* instead.

All six ships were still in service on 19 May 1898, the Edinburgh Holiday, and the following day 'Tantallon' and *Stirling Castle* were drydocked for survey—a routine proceeding. On 23 May they ran steaming trials, and on the following morning sailed straight out of the Forth, never to return. They were to spend the rest of their careers plying out of Constantinople on the Bosphorus ferry services, having been sold to Turkish owners for a total price of £13,150.

Thus, in one day, the Forth lost its entire fleet of Firth cruise ships. With their departure the excursion heyday came to an abrupt end, and though some of the remaining ships were to give many more years of splendid service, never again would the Galloway Saloon Steam Packet Company boast six steamers, or command the public respect it had acquired during its first decade.

Minor Operators

The Galloway fleet did not cater for the small charter party or short distance cruise, and other operators filled these requirements. The firm of J. Henderson and J. McKean operated at Leith throughout the eighties, using *Livingstone* and from 1883 the larger tug *Gladstone*. The former's service in the early 1880s has already been mentioned but she remained available for charters throughout the decade while her consort built up a reasonable short run excursion trade in 1887–89 before being chartered to the Galloway company.

At Charlestown David Wilson used his tug *Boreas* on regatta day excursions from 1876, marking the start of the large fleet of excursion tugs developed by his son and detailed in a later chapter. The same period witnessed the start of the Grangemouth excursion trade with the Mackay brothers and Gabriel Pederson operating *Jupiter* and *Juno*. In 1891 this concern became the Grangemouth Towage Co, and following an amalgamation in 1895 the Grangemouth and Forth Towing Co.

Tourists who travelled to Queensferry by road or rail to view the building of the railway bridge were catered for by Captain Arthur who in 1887 himself built the steam launch *Dalmeny Castle* and offered trips from the harbour around the bridge. She was so successful that the next year he purchased the small paddler *New Undaunted* and both vessels operated until his retirement in 1893.

An Edinburgh doctor, Dr R. Bruce, purchased the yacht *More Vane* in 1886 and attempted to offset her upkeep costs by offering sailings from Granton to Aberdour. With the new Galloway ships in service he soon realised his folly. *More Vane* remained on the Forth as a private yacht till 1891.

Chapter IV

The Railway Ferries

Granton–Burntisland

The Granton–Burntisland ferry began operating on 5 September 1844 and in the same year the Edinburgh & Northern Railway (later the Edinburgh, Perth & Dundee) was promoted. The Duke of Buccleuch had an interest in both concerns. It was natural that on 1 January 1847 railway and ferry should be integrated into a new line of communication to link Edinburgh with Perth and Dundee.

The railways revolutionised the Forth ferries. No longer were the operators dependent on coaches and carts delivering passengers and freight at the ferry slips. Trains, passenger and goods, arrived throughout the day to pour a stream of traffic on to the boats. On the Granton–Burntisland crossing fast passenger boats were supplemented by the first train ferry in the world, *Leviathan*, and other vessels like her. By 1861 the whole ferry operation had been vested in perpetuity in the EP & D and in 1863 the property was inherited by the North British Railway when it absorbed the EP & D.

By 1867 the passage was catering for 92,830 passengers and 50,460 parcels annually. The goods boats carried 90,681 tons of freight and minerals, as well as 1,187 trucks of livestock. At that time the railway fleet consisted of four passenger craft, *Forth, Auld Reekie, Thane of Fife* and *Express*, and five goods boats, *Leviathan, Robert Napier, Carrier, Balbirnie* and *Kinloch*. Of these *Thane of Fife* and *Carrier* usually maintained the Tay crossing at Broughty Ferry while the others were based at Burntisland.

In June 1867 *Dandie Dinmont*, a magnificent saloon steamer built for the Clyde excursions in 1866, was brought to Burntisland but after trials on the ferry service she was laid up as unsatisfactory. Later in the year, however, she was entrusted with the service. A report of 5 November revealed:

The new salooned passenger steamer *Dandie Dinmont*, which has again resumed running, encountered a serious mishap in approaching Burntisland Pier. Hugging the pier too closely she collided with the outer fencing which she brought down on her port sponson, paralysing her paddles and fixing the vessel in the spot she struck. The tide was fortunately full flow, if it had been ebb the steamer could have capsized. Passengers were landed in small boats and the return passage made by goods steamer while another passenger steamer was got ready.

Captain Morrison was cautioned but the Board of Trade considered the elegant 'Dandie' altogether too delicate for the Forth and cancelled her certificate. She was laid up at Burntisland until May 1869 when she was returned to the Clyde.

Another 'stray' was *Carham*, from the NBR Solway Firth fleet. She was brought to the Tay in April 1868, where her lack of saloon facilities caused some criticism, and in June was tried on the Queensferry Passage in the hope that she could succeed an old vessel, *Nymph*. The experiment was not a success, probably she drew too much water for the piers, and she followed 'Dandie' to the Clyde in June 1869.

The ferry operated efficiently but not without incident. *Forth*, while sitting at Burntisland awaiting arrival of the 9.10am train on 27 September 1863, sprang a leak and had to be beached! On 1 February 1867 *Thane of Fife*, on loan from the Tay, broke a paddleshaft in mid-river and reached Burntisland on one paddle. As the spare ship was aground on the mud in the inner harbour a goods steamer had to be commissioned. Two first-class carriages were put on board to serve as deck saloons. Two days later the passenger ferry had to seek the shelter of the goods slip in a gale, while *Kinloch* was blown on to a new slip causing a crane to fall on top of her, staving in her paddlebox! At the end of that month the company was charged in the Sheriff Criminal Court with having run *Thane of Fife* without a certificate. They pleaded guilty, stating in mitigation that the vessel had been brought in an emergency from the Tay and they had neglected to transfer the certificate. They were fined £20 and Captain Morrison £1. In November 1872 the crew of *Balbirnie* broached some whisky casks

Plate 1 A long-vanished landmark, the Newhaven chain pier in its later condition as a sea bathing station and gymnasium
Plate 2 An early excursion favourite, George Jamieson's *Fiery Cross* at Leith Customhouse

Plate 3 The Burntisland – Granton ferry. The goods boat *Midlothian* loading at Burntisland with the *John Stirling* at the ferry pier in the background
Plate 4 On the opening of the Forth railway bridge in 1890 the railway ferries *Auld Reekie, Leviathan, Balbirnie,* and *Kinloch* laid up at Burntisland

but one engineer turned tell-tale and kept his job while the rest of the crew were sacked.

The Alloa Ferry

The ferry at Alloa had fallen into the hands of the Caledonian Railway and had been neglected. Pressure from the Earl of Mar and Kellie forced the company to reintroduce a steamboat on the crossing. In 1869 the Caledonian was contemplating bridging the river and had little interest in the ferry. However, to stave off possible competition the railway company decided to look for a vessel. Several boats were examined and rejected by the Locomotive Superintendent who was authorised to have one built. The result was a small double-bowed paddler named *Countess of Kellie* which arrived at Alloa on 9 December and after having her engines fitted entered service on 24 February 1870. It was reported that 'boat and pier are ill adapted to each other' but the piers were rebuilt later in the year and though a spare vessel was considered the 'Countess' ran alone for the next sixteen years, using salt water in her boiler until pipes were laid to the pier in 1874. A rowing boat, purchased in 1876 for £26, usually acted as spare when she was off, though on at least one occasion the screw steamer *Cameo* was chartered.

With the building of its Alloa railway bridge, the ferry ceased to be of any value to the CR and it gave notice of termination from Whitsunday 1886, the settlement with Mar and Kellie being £246 10s 0d. *Countess of Kellie* was sold to David MacBrayne and converted to a screw steamer to carry coal to the West Highlands.

The ferry lease was taken up by Alex McLeod, an Alloa boat builder, who had a small steam launch, *Lord Erskine*, built at Grangemouth. When traffic was heavy she towed a dumb barge. She remained on this service until replaced by a larger vessel in 1905 and was broken up some time later at the Alloa ferry slip.

North via Queensferry

Construction of a railway from Dunfermline to North Queensferry was approved in 1873. The line, originally in private hands, was acquired by the North British before completion and was opened to traffic on 1 November 1877. The Queensferry Passage became an alternative rail route to the north. A solid stone ferry slip was constructed adjacent to the station at North Queensferry and the ferry called both there and at the Town Pier before crossing the river.

On the south bank, to which the NBR had built a line, construction started again at Port Edgar, where £30,000 was spent on completing the 1,300ft long breakwater and the 900ft jetty. This harbour was opened on 1 October 1878. The steamer thereafter sailed from Port Edgar, calling at the Hawes (Newhalls) for road traffic if the tide was suitable. Calls at Longcraig, which had previously acted as the low water pier, ceased.

In July 1873 the NBR minuted that *Nymph* was under repair and that ferry working was irregular. Two months later Thomas Wheatley, locomotive superintendent, reported that she would not last more than one year. That year, however, passed with no sign of a replacement, the Board of Trade extending *Nymph*'s certificate at a reduced boiler pressure of $6\frac{3}{4}$lb per square inch. This produced insufficient power for her to combat the tides and the service she gave was totally inadequate, but it was December 1875 before serious consideration was given to a replacement.

On 3 February 1875 the NBR locomotive superintendent, now Dugald Drummond, was told to prepare plans for a new tug, but on his own initiative produced a design for a double-sterned, shallow draught screw steamer, specifically planned to meet the requirements of this difficult crossing. She was ordered in May from John Key and Sons of Kinghorn for £5,137. Named *John Beaumont*, she entered service on 2 February 1877.

On New Year's Day 1877 *Nymph* broke her moorings and would have been wrecked had five fishermen not climbed aboard and secured her. They were rewarded with 10s each and on 1 February, with *John Beaumont* ready, *Nymph* was offered for sale. Six weeks later she was withdrawn from the market as the *John Beaumont* had proved to be quite unmanageable, having run aground after a few days in service and being off for repairs until 3 March. Back in service she still proved unsatisfactory, but as her crew got to know her, the problems were partially resolved and in August *Nymph* was again put up for sale. As there were no prospective purchasers Drummond obtained approval to install an old locomotive boiler, and use her as a tug at Charlestown and

Bo'ness. She was again advertised for sale in May 1883, 'lying Port Edgar', but there were no takers and shortly afterwards she was broken up.

John Beaumont again made news on 8 December 1878 by sinking at North Queensferry, but was back in service by the New Year. She was still unsatisfactory. As *Thane of Fife* was surplus to requirements on the Tay she took over the Queensferry Passage on 12 September 1879 and remained its most regular steamer for the next decade.

John Beaumont was converted to paddle propulsion and in her new guise she proved to be a reliable steamer. She was used on the Passage whenever the 'Thane' was required at Burntisland or Tayport, or was off for overhaul. When not in service the 'Johnnie' lay at a mooring in Granton East Harbour.

Preparation for the Tay Bridge

The decision to bridge the Tay and bring the NBR directly into Dundee was taken about 1870. It was a bold move, guaranteed to increase NBR traffic to the North, and while a bridge over the Forth was also contemplated there would be a period where a substantial increase in Forth ferry traffic would have to be catered for. Partly, this would be covered by the rail connections to the Queensferry Passage, but improvements were also deemed necessary on the Burntisland crossing.

In May 1868 the Board of Trade had reduced the number of passengers authorised to be conveyed by the boats, and additional passages had to be laid on. From that date the total capacity of the passenger fleet was required to implement the service. In an accident at Granton on 21 November 1872 *Forth*, backing out from the pier, was so crowded that the helmsman could not see astern and the ship collided with *Kinloch* which was entering the harbour. *Forth* was badly damaged at the stern. The ensuing inquiry found she had been grossly overcrowded and the company was fined £52 10s.

In September 1873 it was minuted that 'the present Forth fleet will suffice for eighteen months' but in July 1874 there were considerable delays in coping with the holiday traffic and consideration was given to purchasing the powerful Clyde steamer *Heather*

Bell; Wheatley also prepared plans for a new steamer and on 14 January 1875 a contract was approved with Key's of Kinghorn at a price of £17,750. On Drummond's appointment a fortnight later the specification was considerably altered, delaying construction for some months, but the ship which finally emerged early in 1876 was a two-funnelled beauty, sturdy, and well suited for the service.

It was originally intended to name her the *Kippendavie* after the NBR chairman's residence, but at her launch she became *John Stirling*, a more direct compliment to the head of the company. With a length of 190ft she was much larger than any of the previous passenger fleet and £2,000 had to be spent in rock blasting at Burntisland pier to provide sufficient water for her at low tide.

In the first season she had a tendency to roll heavily and in November 1876 was fitted with bilge keels as a corrective measure. She was also a wet ship in heavy weather and a large forecastle was added, marring her appearance, but providing useful covered accommodation for livestock and horses.

The goods boats were used for passenger work in emergency, or when traffic was exceptionally heavy. They had no covered accommodation whatsoever. It was accepted that such occasions would increase and in September 1875 an awning was ordered 'for one goods boat when used for passengers—to be made so as to fit all the boats'.

To put the fleet into first class order for the increased traffic, *Kinloch* was reboilered for £3,100 and arrangements made for major renewals to *Express* and *Leviathan*. The latter went to Ramage & Ferguson's Leith Yard in August 1878 for repairs estimated at £2,100 and while there was found to be cracked amidships and requiring considerable strengthening. The workmen went on strike while this was being done, and the repairs were completed by fifteen NBR workmen who were paid by the shipyard.

New boilers were reported as necessary for *Express* in August 1874 but this expense was deferred for as long as possible and in April 1875 she was relegated to spare duties. The contract was given to Key's in January 1878 for £1,220 as the ship was required for the summer traffic. Once the vessel was slipped, very extensive repairs were found to be necessary and in July Key's offer to build a new ferry for £14,250 using the new boilers made for the

Express and taking that ship as £400 of the payment was accepted. Delivery was promised by the end of the year.

Designed round her boilers, this vessel was a smaller version of *John Stirling*, very similar in design, but of neater appearance with closer spaced funnels and smaller paddleboxes. Named *William Muir*, and destined to be the Forth's longest-lived and best-loved paddler, the 'Wullie' got off to a bad start. Once her specification was finalised, delivery was revised to July 1879 but it was October before she was launched with steam up (standard practice at the Kinghorn yard) and immediately entered service.

Forth, the bluff-bowed ugly duckling of the fleet, was immediately sold for £725 to S. & H. Morton of Leith. *William Muir* did not fulfil her contract speed, and the NBR withheld payment of £1,000 to her builders, which was paid, less £134 5s 7d for expenses, in the following September after minor alterations had been made.

The Tay Bridge, designed by Thomas Bouch, was triumphantly opened on 1 June 1878. As expected there was a considerable upsurge in Forth ferry traffic and steamers no longer required on the Tay were brought round to assist.

A skeleton goods service ferry given by the *Robert Napier* was retained between Tayport and Broughty, while *Carrier* came to Burntisland, initially to replace the crippled *Leviathan*, but later to augment the goods fleet. A Tyne tug, *Crow*, was purchased and, renamed *James Cox*, took over the Tay passenger working from August 1879 saving £20 per week, and releasing *Thane of Fife* for the Queensferry Passage. These moves, and the others described, were sufficient to maintain the Forth ferries until the suspension bridge already being built to Bouch's design across the Queensferry narrows would be completed.

Forced Re-organisation

The night of 29 December 1879 completely changed this thinking when the Tay Bridge collapsed with a train on it during a severe gale. On the Forth the ferry that had carried the passengers to their grave was the two-month-old *William Muir*.

Work on the Forth Bridge stopped and *Auld Reekie* went north to Tayport to resume full-scale Tay passenger workings. Goods traffic was diverted via Perth and the Caledonian Railway while plans for rebuilding the Tay Bridge were formulated. *Robert Napier* was converted for use on the bridge reconstruction and when the work was completed, her machinery was removed and she became a coal hulk.

On the Forth the fleet needed reconstruction to see it through a further decade. As noted *John Beaumont* reappeared while Key hurriedly reboilered *Auld Reekie* and *Thane of Fife* for £5,370 each. The latter must have been in poor shape as in March 1881 Key was authorised to spend a further £1,740 on repairs.

Additional goods capacity was urgently required and the specification was prepared in August 1880 for an additional boat. Named *Midlothian* she was built at Leith by Ramage & Ferguson for £27,600 and was in service by the autumn of 1881. No less than 262ft in length, this was by far the largest vessel ever used for service in the Forth. She could carry forty railway wagons and differed in appearance from her predecessors in having her funnel positions reversed (ie fore funnel on the port side, aft one on the starboard). She replaced the small ferry *Carrier*, which was sold complete with gear, and including the cradles, winding gear, engines and boilers from Tayport & Broughty, for £3,400 to S. Mason, an NBR director, who used her to start a vehicular ferry to the Isle of Wight.

Burntisland harbour also received attention and in 1881 a long sea wall was built to provide shelter for both the goods and passenger berths.

The improvements made in the five years up to 1881 increased

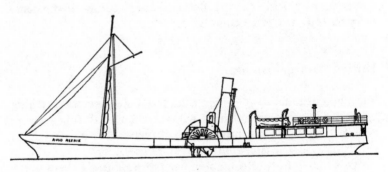

Auld Reekie and *Thane of Fife*

capacity by about 40 per cent. Needless to say, this busy period was not without incident. Off Granton on 17 July 1876 *Kinloch* and the North of Scotland steamer *St Clair* collided, damages being settled in favour of the 'North'. In thick fog on 7 October 1879 *John Stirling* on the 7.20am ex-Granton collided with the steam trawler *Integrity*, the latter sinking in five minutes and the crew of seven being taken to Burntisland by the 'Stirling'. Compensation of £870 plus costs was paid by the railway. Robert Young, the Mate of *Balbirnie*, was killed at Granton in November 1877 when attempting to brake the speed of four wagons being shunted on board.

The Forth Bridge and its Consequences

Work on the famous railway cantilever bridge across the Queensferry narrows started in 1883. During its construction the ferries coped with the expanding railway traffic, mainly due to the opening of the Caledonian Railway's bridge at Alloa in 1886 over which many services were rerouted. The Queensferry bridge was opened by the Prince of Wales on 4 March 1890.

Three excursion steamers ran from Leith, and one from Alloa, all packed with sightseers, while the NBR provided 'one, or if necessary two, Goods Steamers from Burntisland at 10 a.m.' *John Beaumont* and two other small steamers sailed from Queensferry and the Navy's HMS *Jackal* and the lighthouse commissioners' tender *Pharos* were also present, adding authority to the occasion.

After the two special trains had crossed the bridge and the Prince had hammered home a gold-plated rivet, the official party recrossed by sea to view the structure from the water. The Prince of Wales travelled in the builder's little workboat *Dolphin*, 'specially decorated for the occasion in crimson and gold' followed by *William Muir* carrying the guests.

On the following day the Burntisland passenger sailings were reduced to the legal minimum, and maintained by one steamer; the goods boats were withdrawn and laid up at Burntisland. At Queensferry, Port Edgar harbour and station and the railway pier and station at North Queensferry were closed. The ferry was now routed direct between North Queensferry (Town Pier) and the Hawes (Newhalls).

The railway had already decided on 20 February to dispose of all its vessels except *William Muir*, *Thane of Fife* and *Auld Reekie* which were to work the Burntisland, Queensferry and Tayport passages respectively. However, this arrangement was not implemented and on 24 April *John Beaumont* and the lease of the Queensferry Passage were sold for £1,250 to Captain Arthur of South Queensferry. He already operated the small paddler *New Undaunted* (acquired 1887) and the launch *Dalmeny Castle* (1886) from South Queensferry harbour on cruises to the bridge. For the next four summers his augmented fleet gave such excursions every thirty minutes from Hawes Pier, and provided a minimal ferry service.

The Queensferry Passage was leased to John Wilson of Bo'ness in October 1893 when Captain Arthur retired. The NBR provided an annual subsidy of £375, reduced in 1910 to £300, to cover the loss on Forth and Tay and granted Wilson a £1,250 interest-free loan to finance a suitable vessel for Queensferry. He purchased the thirty-two-year-old Tay Ferry *Forfarshire* and she maintained the service for over twenty years, giving frequent cruises round Inchgarvie island to view the bridge, between the official ferry crossings.

From 1890 *William Muir* maintained the Burntisland crossing, and that summer first *Thane of Fife* and later *John Stirling* were chartered for excursion work from Leith.

The sale of the surplus vessels, together with the goods ferry haulage machinery at Burntisland and Granton was approved on 18 September, the lot going to P. & W. MacLellan of Glasgow for £17,250.

The price breakdown was:

Midlothian	£6,750	*Auld Reekie*	£1,000
Kinloch	£1,875	*Thane of Fife*	£1,000
Balbirnie	£1,575	Haulage	
Leviathan	£1,200	machinery	£3,850

John Stirling was kept as spare, but was sold in the spring of 1892 to T. C. Glover, an Edinburgh civil engineer, who appears to have been associated with the Leith shipbuilding firm of S. & H. Morton. At the same time Glover bought *Kinloch*, *Balbirnie* and *Leviathan* from P. & W. MacLellan and these four ships were moved from Burntisland, where they had been laid up, to the Shore at Leith where the three train ferries were broken up later in the year. In 1894 *John Stirling* left for the Manchester Ship Canal, where she operated excursions on charter.

Auld Reekie and *Thane of Fife* went to Norway, leaving the Forth early in 1892. *Thane of Fife* was immediately broken up and *Auld Reekie* sank in 20 fathoms after she sprang a leak in Bergen fairway on 14 September 1893. *Midlothian* outlived the other ferries. Plans to use her to start train ferry services across the Gulf of Mexico, and then in Nigeria fell through. Latterly she belonged to T. W. Ward, the scrap merchant, and at the end of the nineties was sold to Swedish owners, and towed to Scandinavia to be broken up.

Construction of a large wet dock at Burntisland in 1897–1900 involved the complete demolition of the ferry piers and no trace of them now remains. From 1898 *William Muir* used a new passenger slip built on to one of the old coal loading piers. At Granton the slipway used by the passenger boats still remains, but the main high-water pier was used from 1890 by the Lighthouse tender and was largely rebuilt on the appearance of a new *Pharos* in 1909. The goods slip lay immediately landward of this and not a vestige of it survives. Port Edgar was never reopened as a public harbour; it lay derelict until requisitioned by the Admiralty in 1915. Since then it has been a minesweeping base. At North Queensferry the railway pier remained in occasional use, the ferry calling there for coal and water. It again became the ferry terminal in 1920 when a larger boat was put on, and with its later additions to handle car traffic is still intact. It is used as a yachting marina.

Chapter V

Twentieth Century Developments 1898–1918

Troubled Waters

Having sold the two best ships, the Galloway company wasted no time in ordering one replacement for the firth cruises. The tender for £15,686 from John Scott & Company of Kinghorn was accepted and the order placed on 13 July 1898. All the money obtained by the sale of the two vessels was thus reinvested, but it was hoped that a substantial saving would be made in operating costs. Meanwhile the company operated a policy of 'make do and mend' and the Alloa tug *Flying Bat* was chartered from 16 July to 4 September and allocated to the Aberdour/Queensferry runs along with the two 'Lords', while the ageing *Wemyss Castle* was promoted to firth cruise ship, on a modified roster including a variety of day and afternoon sailings.

It was a fine summer and by late July there were complaints that the Aberdour vessels could not handle the traffic. The 'Wemyss' was recalled to increase capacity, *Lord Aberdour* transferred to the Stirling run, and 'Edinburgh' placed on the firth cruises. She returned occasionally with a seasick complement, while *Lord Aberdour*'s poor amenities and lack of catering deterred many upriver travellers. Nor was the Aberdour service improved; *Lord Morton* developed boiler trouble which put her out of service on several occasions, and towards the end of the season the 'Wemyss' was withdrawn to have her cylinder rebored and a new piston fitted. The Board realised that drastic action was required, and on 11 August a second order was placed with Scott's, for a general purpose steamer at a cost of £11,791. As delivery was promised by May 1899, it was agreed not to recommission the worn out *Lord Aberdour*.

The first of the new ships was launched with steam up on 6 May and named *Tantallon Castle*. Scott promised delivery of the second ship by July, but it was 7 October before she was launched and named *Stirling Castle*. Due to this late delivery the 1899 services had to be improvised, with unfortunate results.

The firth cruises were adequately covered by the new 'Tantallon', and the Stirling run by *Edinburgh Castle*. To assist on the Aberdour/Queensferry runs *Flying Bat* was again chartered from mid-July to the end of August. Both *Lord Morton* and *Wemyss Castle* developed boiler trouble and all too frequently the other steamers had to rescue stranded passengers late in the evening. The company's reputation sank and on 1 August the Board, in an attempt to retrieve the situation, agreed to reboiler and lengthen *Lord Morton*, and carry out extensive repairs to *Wemyss Castle*.

The new *Tantallon Castle*, with a length of 210ft, was by far the largest vessel the company had owned to date, and with twin funnels and her paddles set well aft was a really handsome ship. Her compound machinery gave a speed of $16\frac{1}{2}$ knots, and there was ample accommodation with a Class 3 certificate for 787

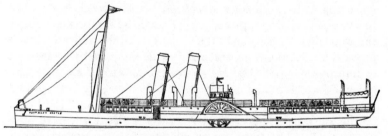

Tantallon Castle of 1899

passengers. Furnishings were lavish. The first-class main saloon was divided into three elliptical alcoves on each side, with walls panelled in solid oak, surmounted by an egg and dart cornice also in oak. The alcoves were separated by Greek carved pilasters, with capitals in walnut, inlaid with gold. The ceiling was white and gold, the couches upholstered in gold Utrecht velvet, and at the after end were stained-glass windows.

Internally *Stirling Castle* was a miniature version of her big sister with similar lavish fittings and gold upholstery. Her single funnel was telescopic and her mast hinged. To give maximum manoeuvrability her compound machinery was disconnecting and she could turn in her own length when required. She proved to be one of the most useful and versatile vessels the company ever possessed.

Lord Morton's new boiler was fitted in April 1900 by Hawthorn & Company at Granton, and she was lengthened by 12ft directly behind the engine room. These alterations cost £2,067 and eliminated the ship's earlier tendency to sail down by the head. New funnels of greater diameter considerably enhanced her appearance, and she returned to service a better ship in every respect. The old *Lord Aberdour* was traded in as part payment for this work and was broken up at Granton in the autumn.

This modernisation programme should have resulted in a first-class fleet but its effect was marred when *Tantallon Castle* turned out a failure. Her designers, in their anxiety to ensure that she was not bow heavy, had erred too far in the opposite direction and the vessel had insufficient weight forward, making her lively and alarmingly slow to answer the helm.

Entering Leith on 28 June 1899 she was unable to avoid the departing Gibson steamer *Abbotsford* which struck her on the forward port sponson, piercing her diagonally for nine feet above the waterline. Repairs took ten days. Her lifeboats were moved forward to the sponsons, and steady sails fitted, but this attempt to improve her trim had little effect. The long cruises she had given in June to the Farne Islands and Dundee were not repeated and the ship was thereafter kept within the confines of the Firth. In the autumn of 1900 a new rudder was fitted but gave little improvement. The company was glad to sell her when an offer of £15,250 was received from Hawthorn Bros of London in April 1901.

Tenders for a replacement were considered on 6 August, including a bid from the Parsons Marine Steam Turbine Company. A turbine ship seemed the ideal answer for firth work. The Directors had been watching the performance of the prototype *King Edward* very closely on the Clyde, and M. P. Galloway was instructed to enter into detailed negotiations with Parsons.

With this ship in mind Aitken & Galloway had another look at Portobello pier. It had never been designed to take the strain of such a large vessel, and for screw propulsion there was insufficient water at low spring tides. They decided to build a wooden extension, seaward and separate from the pier. It was triangular in shape giving two berths, sheltered respectively from east and west winds, and connected to the pier by gangways. It was erected during the winter of 1901–2 at a cost of £2,152 15s 1d.

But negotiations were abruptly terminated on 25 September 1901 due to a financial crisis and the turbine was never built. Andrew Wallace was responsible, the trouble going back to the NBR share purchase of 1889. At that time Aitken and Galloway had left Andrew, and his brother, Dr John, holding a 37½ per cent minority interest, and he had never forgiven them. Throughout 1890–1 he had fought tooth and nail for what he believed to be just, arguing that railway operation by nominee shareholders was illegal. The meetings became slanging matches with Wallace objecting to the purchase of Portobello pier and *Wemyss Castle*, and hurling abuse at his co-directors, then walking out in disgust. He and his brother had refused to pay the share call issued in July 1891 and the company sued them, winning their case. Andrew resigned from the Board on 30 November the same year and took no further interest in the company. No trouble was therefore anticipated when the call for the balance of £2 2s 6d per share was issued in April 1900. Unexpectedly, Andrew and his late brother's executors again refused to pay and after considerable procrastination offered their shares for sale to the company.

By 1900 Mr Simpson, the NBR general accountant, was unhappy about the Galloway company. Here was a concern whose dividend rarely, if ever, covered the interest charges on the loan which financed it, and yet was currently spending money at a rate quite disproportionate to its earning capacity. Its operators, Aitken and Galloway, both had other substantial outside business commitments. The Steam Packet Company was their hobby.

In December 1900 the NBR Board formally expressed 'extreme dissatisfaction with the accounts', and when the Wallace shares were offered back they instructed the company to accept them. They also insisted that minor holdings held by Aitken, Galloway, and others were returned at the same time. The railway declined to purchase these shares and refused to allow them to be resold. £16,180 was paid out and in effect reduced the company's capital from £43,160 to £26,980. The NBR (through its nominees) was

63

the sole remaining shareholder and no funds were now available for a turbine, or for that matter, any other new steamer.

A Fight for Survival

In December 1901 the NBR sought a detailed explanation of the GSSP's accounts. M. P. Galloway managed to avoid answering for a year but eventually was forced to reply. The accountant's suspicion that the Steam Packet Company had little prospect of earning money was confirmed. On 26 March 1903 the full NBR board minuted its approval 'of the proposed dissolution of the co-partnership styled The Galloway Saloon Steam Packet Company'. The Steam Packet board meeting on 29 July was called to implement this decision, but Galloway so eloquently presented the prospects for the future, with ships in use all year as 'liberty boats' for the new naval dockyard at Rosyth, that he swayed George Wieland, of the NBR, and the Board agreed to 'continue running the boats till the end of the season, unless sold'. While the Rosyth traffic never materialised a good summer generated excursion traffic and in November the company declared a 5 per cent dividend.

There was no further talk of liquidation. Instead the NBR now embarked on a policy of milking its subsidiary of its fluid reserves. In April 1904 Galloway was told to lend £2,000 to the NBR, an instruction he did not carry out. The NBR then had the constitution altered to give its board power to reduce the Galloway capital at any time they wished. In the following month a reduction of £8,000 was agreed, the money to be returned to the NBR. The railway and Galloway books were adjusted accordingly, but Aitken and Galloway did not send the money. They were still thirled to the idea of a screw steamer and while they had insufficient capital for a turbine, they might well, by using this £8,000, scrape up enough for a more modest vessel.

The opportunity to seek such a ship occurred in 1905, following the death of George Wieland. Aitken informed the NBR board that *Wemyss Castle* would be unfit for service by September and proposed financing a twin-screw reciprocating steamer for firth cruises from the company's depreciation fund. The plans were submitted to the NBR, and approved by Dr Inglis, an NBR director and proprietor of the Clyde shipbuilding and engineering firm of A. & J. Inglis.

An order was placed with Hawthorn's of Leith in August, at a price of £12,210 12s 11d and *Wemyss Castle* sold for scrap, realising the princely sum of £475. At her launching on 13 February 1906 the new ship was named *Roslin Castle* and on 2 May she ran her trials. The press then extolled the virtues of screw propulsion and the 'Roslin' quickly became a very popular ship with good looks, seaworthiness, and a high standard of accommodation which was improved in her second season by the addition of a deck cabin and companionway over the main saloon entrance.

Considering the company's state of health, the service offered to the public in the 1900s was remarkably good. With five ships, the 1900 service closely resembled that of the nineties, the new 'Tantallon' and 'Stirling' taking over their predecessors' duties with the exception that the latter, on Sundays, sandwiched a run via Bo'ness and Kincardine to Alloa or the Windings, in between her morning and evening Methil service. On weekdays the capacities of the enlarged *Lord Morton* and *Wemyss Castle* were sufficient for the Aberdour and Queensferry services, and at the weekends they were assisted by *Edinburgh Castle*, which served Stirling during the week.

From 1901 the *Stirling Castle* handled the firth work alone, and performed very well, with regular cruises going as far as the Carr lightship. On Sundays she served both Kirkcaldy and Methil and performed the Windings cruises. With only one cruise ship available, calls at the smaller ports were abandoned; Largo, Anstruther, and Dunbar disappearing from the sailing bills while the Stirling run was speeded up by omitting Bo'ness and Charlestown. This allowed *Edinburgh Castle* to do some general cruising and her day's work now often included a Bass Rock cruise in addition to the up-river service.

In 1901 only, when an additional ship was still a possibility, the up-river service started from Portobello to compensate for the lack of the second firth cruise, and *Flying Bat* was chartered to supplement the Aberdour/Queensferry services, opening her season with unusual cruises round Inchkeith from Portobello. On her arrival in 1906 *Roslin Castle* took over the firth schedules while *Stirling Castle* was transferred upriver, and the 'Edinburgh' took over from *Wemyss Castle*.

On the discontinuing of calls at Largo the gangway there was moved to Aberdour and placed just east of the Hawkcraig pier. Sunday low water landings were thereafter made with the ship tied up at the closed Hawkcraig pier, while the passengers were floried from the seaward side of the vessel to the gangway.

Ferry Improvements

While thinking of liquidating its Galloway subsidiary, the NBR decided to improve the Burntisland ferry, and operate it in summer as an excursion service. *William Muir* was repainted in 1902, in the attractive Clyde steamer livery of red funnels with white bands and black tops, and gilt lines were painted along her hull.

By 1910 *William Muir* was worn out after thirty-four years of continuous service, relieved since 1892 for only a short spell each spring by the Galloway *Wemyss Castle* (*Edinburgh Castle* from 1906). Early that year she retired to Ramage & Ferguson's yard at Leith for complete mechanical renewal and emerged almost beyond recognition. The fore-funnel and forward boiler room had gone, the space having been utilised to provide extra deck area for road vehicles. She was given a new compound diagonal engine with steam supplied from twin cylindrical boilers astern of the engines. New small paddlewheels and boxes had also been fitted and she was now good for another quarter-century of work.

On the Queensferry Passage *Forfarshire* was reboiled in 1904 and her funnel substantially lengthened, giving her an altogether odd appearance. In 1908 the service was augmented by the acquisition of *Woolwich*, an eighteen-year-old cast-off from the London County Council. Her arrival allowed the ferry to handle road vehicles all the year round, with the duties shared between the newcomer and the veteran *Forfarshire*.

At Alloa, ferry traffic from the sawmills at South Alloa was increasing and in 1905 a larger vessel was provided. This was *Hope*, a 63ft twin-screw steamer, locally built and destined to serve on the crossing for the next thirty years. In the mornings girls from Airth and Throsk used her to reach Alloa Glass Works, and the crossing, while very short, could be dangerous. *Hope* was often carried by the tide several miles up or down stream, and on foggy

Plate 5 Low tide at Portobello. The 1899 *Stirling Castle* moored below the pier restaurant
Plate 6 The Galloway flagship, the 1887 *Tantallon Castle* at May Island

Plate 7 Lord Morton at Aberdour in the 1890s arriving at the Stone pier
Plate 8 The *Stirling Castle* of 1899 leaving North Berwick

mornings the first advice the Alloa slip master had of her approach
was a chorus of female voices singing:

> McLeod's got a ferry,
> The ferry's got a bell,
> And every time the fog comes down,
> Sailor rings his bell.

The Bo'ness Steamers

On both shores of the river upstream were sizeable industrial
populations and the workers sought escape from their harsh
working environment via the harbours of Bo'ness and Charlestown. These workers regarded the Galloway ships as for 'toffs'
and had their own fleet in the excursion tugs owned by John S.
Wilson of Bo'ness. Known as 'Tugboat', Wilson had a collection
of antiquated craft, most of which, however, possessed passenger
certificates and operated charters or excursions. They were:

Name	Built	Owned	Notes
Boreas	1872	1876–1898	Charlestown tug
Sea King	1860	1884–1892	
Admiral	1876	1888–1918	Bo'ness tug
Venus	1868	1890–1902	
Dolphin	1885	1890–1919	Tayport ferry steamer
Forfarshire	1861	1893–1919	Queensferry ferry steamer
Thomas and Mary	1857	1893–1894	Burntisland tug
Dalmeny Castle	1887	1893–1895	Passenger launch
Royal Norman	1881	1896–1919	Bo'ness tug
Grappler	1884	1896–1911	
Lord Elgin	1867	1898–1900	Charlestown tug
Conquest	1867	1899–1914	
Pero Gomez	1869	1902–1919	Burntisland tug
Clutha No. 6	1884	1904–1917	Excursion steamer
Flying Fish	1882	1906–1919	
Woolwich	1890	1908–1919	Queensferry ferry steamer
Betefdoe	1875	1913–1915	
The Earl	1872	1914–1919	⎫ No passenger
Dredger No. 1	1871	1918–1919	⎭ certificate

Royal Norman was the best-known vessel at Bo'ness, and throughout the season provided afternoon or evening cruises each Wednesday and Saturday. On Wednesday evenings there was also a cruise from the Hawes Pier, South Queensferry, where *Admiral* or *Pero Gomez* were the usual vessels. If the passenger complement was within their Class 4 certificate the sail was usually down Firth; if there were too many on board for this, the ship cruised upriver to Brucehaven or Bo'ness. On rare occasions when there were altogether too many passengers for the tug, the cruise was taken by the ferry *Forfarshire*.

During the July Bo'ness holidays excursions were given daily, and it required three vessels to handle this traffic. Destinations ranged from Stirling, to as far down the firth as Elie Point or the May Island. (From 1911 they were restricted to within Class 4 limits.) In the same week South Queensferry was busy with visitors down to see the bridge, and a fourth vessel was employed from Hawes Pier cruising 'to various places of interest within the firth' while a fifth ship ranged the firth, bringing visitors to Bo'ness. The ships took a short rest the following week, and their normal programme was resumed once the local workers had received their post-holiday pay packet.

In arranging his programme Wilson demonstrated something of the flair Jamieson had shown at Leith in earlier years. There was a cruise for every conceivable occasion. The Stirling and Alloa Games, the fairs at Kincardine and Culross, the regatta at South Queensferry and the Kirkcaldy band contest were all covered. On Coronation Day in 1911 there was a sailing to Inchkeith 'to view the bonfires along the shores', and two years later *Flying Fish* sailed to Portobello, with the Linlithgow Pipe Band, on an organised visit to the local pottery. There was even a cruise from Alloa to Bo'ness for a bowling match, on which a gentleman slipped off the gangplank into the water and was stated to have 'skinned his collar'. That Wilson could also be generous is shown by a 1908 evening cruise to Charlestown accompanied by the Kinneil Band, with the entire proceeds going 'for the benefit of Andrew McLaren, Blacksmith, who has been unable to work for the last two years'.

The acquisition of *Clutha No. 6*, a Clyde river 'bus', in September 1904 was a major step in Wilson's excursion operations. She was the only purely pleasure craft ever owned by him. She was useful in the Windings where, being double-ended, she could reverse all the way to Alloa. In her first season, she operated daily from Grangemouth giving cruises to the Windings, Culross, the training ship *Caledonia* at Queensferry, and even to Bo'ness. These sailings were not repeated in future years though it is from 1905 to 1912 that Wilson's pleasure sailings were at their maximum.

From 1905 the new naval dockyard at Rosyth provided a popular focal point for many a short cruise:

> *Royal Norman* cast away from Bo'ness with a gladsome complement 200 strong—the turn round tour—of the naval base and Forth Bridge. The Woodbines were flourished with much gusto. They generally are upon occasions so auspicious—the shilling walking stick, complete with polished mountings,—indispensible items both in the outfit of a globe trotter. The spy glasses handed down from the last generation must make an appearance . . .

The Marine Gardens at Portobello also proved a big attraction when they were opened in 1909 and thereafter Leith became the most frequent cruise destination, the journey to Portobello being completed by tramcar.

Charters were also popular, and most were open to the public. They were usually organised by the various church Sabbath Schools or Choirs; the Old Boy's Athletic FC, the Rechabites, Good Templars, or the YMCA. The growth of the latter organisation was dramatic; in 1906 *Clutha* took them to Alloa; by 1913 it required the combined capacities of *Royal Norman*, *Flying Fish* and the Alloa tug *Flying Bat* to convey them to Burntisland.

Soon after the White Star liner *Titanic* sank in mid-Atlantic, *Admiral* ran on the rocks off the Hawes pier. There was consternation on board, but the passengers got safely ashore. *Titanic*, however, put an end to Wilson's excursion business, as following the disaster the Board of Trade introduced new safety regulations, requiring additional life-saving equipment on all passenger vessels. Wilson was not prepared to spend this money on his ageing fleet, and the excursions came to an abrupt end in mid-July 1913.

Excursions round the Forth Bridge from Hawes Pier were resumed in 1914, given by *Electric Arc*, a small launch owned by the Scottish Motor Traction Company which had been operating a motor bus service from Edinburgh to the bridge since 1906, and had decided it would increase the traffic if it could offer its own cruises. *Electric Arc* had been built at Dumbarton in 1911 to the order of Mr Mavor of Mavor & Coulson, and is believed to have been the first electrically propelled boat in the world.

Grangemouth and Kirkcaldy

Compared with the activities of the Bo'ness fleet, the programme offered by the Grangemouth & Forth Towing Company was meagre. It consisted of the dozen or so afternoon and evening cruises given annually by *Jupiter* from her berth in the Old Dock, Grangemouth, at the foot of Grange Street, and most sailings had a connecting train from Falkirk (Grahamston). The season started in late May and there were daily sailings during the Falkirk Trades in early July.

In 1902 *Forth* (a sister vessel to the Alloa *Flying Bat*) was fitted with deck seating and a canvas awning, and took over this excur-

Jupiter in the Windings

72

sion work, *Jupiter*'s certificate being allowed to lapse. Thereafter there was a long midsummer gap in the sailings, as from about 10 July till the end of August *Forth* was stationed at Berwick-upon-Tweed to tow the fishing fleet in and out of the river. She gave cruises along the Northumberland and Berwickshire coasts.

As at Bo'ness, public charter sailings were common, usually being organised by the church groups. Two steamers were frequently required, and either Wilson's *Flying Fish* or the Alloa *Flying Bat* assisted. They also handled any charters required while *Forth* was at Berwick.

Flying Bat was also chartered to the Grangemouth & Forth Company during the Falkirk Trades in 1904, 1907, 1911 and 1914, when she assisted the *Forth* with cruises to the Windings and to Leith. McLeod's operated her itself on the weekend of 24/5 July 1909 on sailings between Leith, Portobello and Kirkcaldy, and throughout 1910 when she sailed daily from Leith to Alloa and the Windings. Similar cruises were given from Bo'ness during the 1912 holidays, in opposition to Wilson's steamers.

Kirkcaldy enjoyed a Sunday service by the Galloway steamers until the summer of 1907. The following season this was taken over by the Kirkcaldy Towing Company using its tug *Fifeshire* and she maintained it until 1914, sailing on Sundays throughout the season and daily during the Edinburgh holidays. On Fife holidays she cruised from Kirkcaldy to Aberdour, Rosyth Dockyard or the Forth Bridge.

A New Galloway Era

Thomas Aitken died in February 1907. He was one of Leith's foremost shipping personalities, chairman of the London & Edinburgh Shipping Company and of the Galloway Saloon Steam Packet Company. For the latter concern, his death marked the end of the era of independence, and the NBR appointed its director, Henry Grierson, as his successor.

Grierson's policy was to contain the company within limits which did not compete with the railway, to make it profitable, and to release as much capital as possible for railway use. He discontinued the Stirling run, and *Stirling Castle* was sold in March to Southampton owners for £8,750. This money was loaned to the

NBR. He also decreed that the steamers would carry no luggage—it should be sent in advance by rail unless it was destined for the hotel and tearoom adjacent to the Hawkcraig pier at Aberdour.

A critical investigation of the accounts followed. The non-payment of the £8,000 in 1904 was discovered, and the capital account adjusted. The investigation also showed that the company was paying dearly for many of its supplies (notably coal which the same vendor sold to the railway at a substantially lower price) and where appropriate, bulk purchasing was arranged through the railway.

In March 1908 the Admiralty was scouring the country for vessels for use as fleet tenders. It acquired the Clyde steamer *Strathmore* and put in an offer of £15,000 for *Roslin Castle*. As this was 32 per cent over her building cost it was too good an offer to turn down and she became the fleet tender HMS *Nimble*. Tenders for her replacement were examined on 22 September but the Board decided there was insufficient capital available and turned them down. It agreed, however, to install electric lighting in *Edinburgh Castle* to allow firth evening cruise work to be resumed, and a fortnight later accepted on terms to be agreed, a Clyde steamer which the NBR stated would be surplus in 1909.

This turned out to be *Redgauntlet* which had been built for the NBSP in 1895, and was typical of the Clyde fleet. Her career had been unfortunate, and almost ended in August 1899 when she grounded on rocks at the south end of Arran. Repairs cost over £5,000 and appeared not to have been entirely satisfactory as she was thereafter employed on calm water routes, and since 1906 had been spare steamer. She was not the ideal choice for Forth cruising, though compared with the other members of the fleet was powerful and well appointed. The powerful 'slap' of her paddle beat and her surging wash are still recalled by those who can remember her.

She arrived at Leith in March 1909 in NBR colours and for her work with Galloway only the funnel livery was altered. This became the familiar navy yellow, but the railway black top was retained. Expenditure was kept to a minimum but before entering service, arrangements were made to improve her electric lighting, install a steam windlass and capstan, and fit a brake cylinder to her starting engine. The NBR was paid a transfer price of £4,000.

In view of her past history trouble was to be expected, and in

January 1910 the Board read a sombre report on her condition. The short, sharp seas of the firth had done their work, and hull flexing had slackened rivets to an alarming extent. Considerable stiffening was required to make her seaworthy and S. & H. Morton's tender of £1,150 was accepted. This work included the fitting of a small forecastle to stiffen the bow and built on this was a landing platform for use at May Island. Thus refitted, the ship gave sterling service and the popularity of her cruises increased each year.

Her livery proved much less expensive to maintain than the yacht finish on the other vessels, and late in 1910 the top portion of their funnels were repainted black. For the 1911 season their hulls also became black, though the white saloons and paddle-boxes were retained.

Throughout Grierson's chairmanship the regular Aberdour and Queensferry steamers were *Edinburgh Castle* and *Lord Morton*. In 1907 *Roslin Castle* helped out on busy Saturdays, but spent most of her time on cruises. These included a few calls at Anstruther, and on the Falkirk holiday she gave a special sailing from Grangemouth. There were no firth cruises in 1908 and no calls were made at any of the piers, with the exception of Methil. To relieve pressure on the Aberdour route and allow *Edinburgh Castle* to maintain a Sunday run to Methil, *Flying Bat* was again chartered—for the May holiday, Trades week, and every Saturday and Sunday throughout July and August.

After the arrival of *Redgauntlet* cruises were given more regularly than before, and though variations were introduced from time to time the following example from 1909 is typical: Day cruise via Portobello, Methil, and Elie on Mondays, Tuesdays, Thursdays and Fridays to (Mon) The North Carr Light or St Andrews; (Tues) North Berwick and the Bass Rock; (Thur and Fri) North Berwick and May Island. A double run was given to North Berwick and the Bass Rock on Wednesdays and to Elie on Saturdays while on Sundays *Redgauntlet* maintained the Methil service with an afternoon cruise round the Bass Rock. There was no weekend assistance available for the Aberdour Passage and on Saturdays the service was speeded up by omitting all calls at Queensferry, though the steamer still sailed triangularly via the Forth Bridge.

Upriver cruises, via Queensferry, Bo'ness and Kincardine,

were reintroduced in 1911, replacing the Sunday Bass Rock cruises. Dependent on the tide they either terminated at Alloa or continued to the Windings. In the latter case they were given by *Edinburgh Castle* which was the only ship able to pass the Alloa bridge, and on those days *Redgauntlet* sailed to Aberdour. The other cruises were by *Redgauntlet* and on a morning tide she sailed early from Leith to give a cruise from Alloa via all the piers to Methil and the Bass Rock, while her return journey was advertised as an evening cruise from Leith. On this service she often steamed against the strong river tide, something few of her predecessors had been scheduled to do.

Some of the enterprising spirit of earlier days was now returning and the public reciprocated by giving its patronage. At the close of the 1912 season the company reported its highest passenger receipts for many years. In these improved conditions Grierson was able to achieve his ambition of releasing money for railway use and the capital was reduced by £20,000 to £6,980. The money (£8,750 of which was already on loan) was returned to the NBR which now viewed the Steam Packet Company as a useful asset.

Expansion and Competition

Galloway company policy now moved towards expansion. With only three steamers it had been unable to accept many charter sailings, but from 1913 the company took all that were offered, chartering *Flying Bat* (and in 1914 also *Forth*) to maintain the scheduled Aberdour service.

Calls at Kirkcaldy were also resumed in 1913, when during the Fife holidays *Flying Bat* was stationed there for cruises to Inchkeith, the Forth Bridge and Portobello. In 1914 sailings were given on the Falkirk May and July holiday Mondays (two ships from Grangemouth) and for the full duration of the Bo'ness holiday. On Edinburgh Trades Monday *Redgauntlet* preceded her cruise with a YMCA charter sailing from Bo'ness to Kirkcaldy and both tugs were on charter that week giving a half-hourly cruise service from Portobello round Inchkeith.

Extra lifeboats were provided on *Redgauntlet* and *Edinburgh Castle* in 1914 to meet the new Board of Trade regulations, and in

February the Board agreed, subject to railway approval, to purchase the magnificent Dundee-based paddler *Slieve Bearnagh* for a maximum of £8,000. The NBR, however, did not approve and other steamers were then considered. *Mavis*, operating on the Bristol Channel, was turned down in April, as was the offer of the Kirkcaldy Towing Company's *Fifeshire*. Another project mooted was for a pier at Leven as the dock extension opened the previous year at Methil had made that call rather unattractive. A pier at the resort was now deemed necessary but construction was deferred while the Burgh Council discussed the dredging of the River Leven with the NBR.

A change of management had been responsible for this dynamic outlook. By 1913 John Galloway Galloway was keenly interested in the company and he succeeded as manager following his father's death at the age of seventy on 10 November. Grierson's death followed two months later, on 26 January 1914, and Bruce Gilroy was then appointed chairman.

By this time the possibility of competition was very real, as a number of town councils, alienated by the earlier reduction in services, had got together and under the chairmanship of Brigadier-General Sir Robert Cranston, a well-known figure and former Lord Provost of Edinburgh, formed The Forth Pleasure Sailings Company in October 1913. Queensferry and Kirkcaldy were strongly represented, but Stirling decided not to subscribe after having been assured by Galloway that a specification for a new up-river steamer was ready.

Slieve Bearnagh, rejected by the NBR in February 1914, was brought to the Forth by her Dundee owner, Messrs D. & J. Nicol. Advertised as 'the largest pleasure steamer on the east coast' she sailed between Kirkcaldy and Leith on 8 July, before giving an evening cruise from Kirkcaldy. These sailings were repeated the following day and on the 10th she gave an evening cruise from Leith to the Bass Rock. She then went back to Dundee for the local holidays but as soon as they were over returned to Kirkcaldy and on 1 August took up daily sailings to Leith and round the Bass Rock.

These developments thoroughly alarmed the NBR and when the Aberdour pier lease was renewed, a clause was inserted that the Earl of Morton would grant no similar rights to competitors; at Bo'ness the charges for passengers landing from non-railway steamers were greatly increased. Even though war had broken out with Germany the NBR instructed the Galloway Company to obtain a new vessel for its firth work for the 1915 season. A tender from the Ailsa yard at Troon for a duplicate of the Bristol Channel *Glen Usk* was considered in September 1914, but deferred while the company unsuccessfully attempted to purchase *Slieve Bearnagh* for £4,000. The NBR then entered into negotiations with A. & J. Inglis of Glasgow for two steamers, one for Galloway and one for its Clyde fleet. This order was placed in October, with delivery of the Forth ship—at a cost of no less than £27,500—promised for May 1915. In November, the Duke of Buccleuch having been appointed a director, it was agreed that the new vessel be named *Duchess of Buccleuch*. In February 1915 an estimate was obtained for dredging and alterations at the Hawes Pier to allow the excursion steamers to call, but due to hostilities the work was deferred.

The Great War

One can speculate endlessly on what form the 1915 excursion programme might have taken. It would have been exciting with three companies in competition but it was not to be, for from midnight on 2 August 1914 the Admiralty declared the Forth estuary a controlled area, with excursion sailings prohibited. On 4 August, by which time we were at war with Germany, sailings after dark were prohibited on the Burntisland ferry, and on 13 August the Queensferry Passage was reduced to three crossings per day.

Slieve Bearnagh returned to Dundee and the Galloway fleet was laid up at Port Edgar. *Duchess of Buccleuch* was never delivered, being requisitioned while still on the stocks, and completed in April 1916 as a fleet minesweeper. The company received £3,550 compensation in February 1917. By April 1915 a military billet was established on the sea end of Portobello pier, and in June 1916 Port Edgar was taken over as a minesweeping base. *Redgauntlet* had already departed for minesweeping on 23 May. *Edinburgh Castle* and *Lord Morton* were moved to Bo'ness but on 28 June they, too, were requisitioned. The Admiralty offer to pay charter of £85 a month for *Redgauntlet* and £10 for each of the others was rejected by the company. Much haggling followed with the GSSP claiming grossly inflated values for its fleet, but agreement was finally reached at a meeting in London on 12 August 1917 when the Admiralty purchased the three ships for £16,933 6s 8d. None ever returned to the Forth. After the war *Redgauntlet* was sold to French interests in Algeria, while the other two were converted into hospital ships to support the expeditionary force fighting the Russian Bolsheviks. Both were blown up in the White Sea to avoid capture on 24 September 1919. No post-war employment could be found for *Duchess of Buccleuch* and she was laid up until 1921 when she was broken up at Llanelly. *Slieve Bearnagh* also became a minesweeper and hospital carrier, afterwards being laid up at Inverkeithing until broken up in 1923.

Operation of the Burntisland ferry became increasingly difficult as the war progressed and at Granton *William Muir* (*Edinburgh Castle* in April 1915 and 1916) had to thread her way through an increasing maze of minesweepers, fleet trawlers, and patrol boats. From 1 January 1917 the ferry was suspended on Admiralty orders. *William Muir* was later requisitioned for minesweeping duties and served at Sheerness from June 1917 till May 1919. Her Master, Captain Clark, went on service with her.

Late in 1917 Portobello Pier was declared unsafe and on 17 January 1918 the Galloway company accepted an offer to demolish it for £2,180. It came down that spring. By this time both the Hawkcraig Pier at Aberdour and the railway pier at North Queensferry had also been requisitioned though the ferry was still allowed to use the latter for coaling and watering. The Town Pier approach was dredged and the pier repaired by the Admiralty to allow the ferry to use it for all service sailings.

The only civilian services were the Alloa and Queensferry ferries. On the latter, traffic had picked up quickly with the increased naval activity at Rosyth and from 1 January 1915 Wilson agreed to work it without a subsidy. The Admiralty later increased its 'liberty' service to Rosyth and the subsidy was restored at the increased figure of £375 per annum from 1 July 1917. Increased operating costs soon made this an unrealistic figure and from 1 July 1918 it was increased to £1,000 per annum.

One of the vessels used on the Rosyth liberty run was the SMT launch *Electric Arc*. She was also the fleet mail boat and was on

this duty when fire broke out one morning and her blazing hulk
was beached near Port Edgar. Hawes Pier was used by the liberty
service and in January 1918 the Admiralty decided to dredge an
approach and extend the pier by 16ft to provide a low-water
landing. The NBR agreed on the condition that its Galloway
fleet would have access. This extension was completed but never
used, the Rosyth traffic going via Port Edgar which the Admiralty
purchased in 1920.

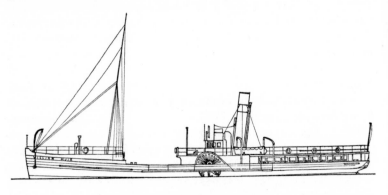

William Muir as altered 1910

Chapter VI

A Twilight Interlude
1919–1945

1919

William Muir completed her Admiralty service in May 1919 and, after a hurried refit, reopened the Forth Ferry (as the Burntisland Ferry was now called) on 16 July, the week before the Edinburgh holidays. She was based at Granton and made four double crossings on weekdays and three on Sundays. The only other sailings from Edinburgh that summer were on the Trades Monday, Tuesday and Wednesday and the September holiday Monday when the Grangemouth & Forth company's tug *Forth* cruised to the Forth Bridge from the Victoria Jetty, Leith (the West Pier was being used by the navy).

Forth had reappeared in her summer finery for the Falkirk holidays on 1 July, when she cruised daily from Grangemouth to Leith and Aberdour. For the rest of the season, cruises from Grangemouth were more regular than in pre-war years and included one call at Queensferry, the last to be made by a passenger ship at that burgh's pier.

There were no services by the Galloway Saloon Steam Packet Company, whose entire assets comprised the piers at Hawkcraig Aberdour, North Berwick and Elie, ticket boxes at Methil and Elie and a flory boat at Aberdour. All were in poor condition, and although the NBR had a spare steamer on the Clyde, it was decided not to restart the Forth services. The piers were advertised for sale but there were no takers and the leases were cancelled in February 1921, when the Earl of Morton was paid £1,200 in lieu of repairs at Aberdour. The company then went into voluntary liquidation.

John S. Wilson, lessee of the Queensferry and Tayport passages, died at Bo'ness on 3 February 1919. His executors continued the business for a few months but on 30 September sold out to the recently formed Leith Salvage and Towage Company, itself an amalgamation of various interests, and owner of the *Fifeshire*, which had operated to Kirkcaldy in pre-war days. The company never entered the excursion business, but, in the early twenties tugs were available for charter sailings, one example being the picnic of the 1st Leith Boys' Brigade by *Cambria* to Inchcolm on 9 September 1922.

Ferry Reorganisation

Increased operating costs soon convinced the Leith Salvage and Towage Company that it was undesirable to continue the ferry leases, and in the autumn of 1920 the company requested the NBR to relieve it of these obligations. The Tayport crossing ceased in October, and after an unsuccessful attempt to obtain another lessee, the NBR took over the working of the Queensferry Passage on 13 November.

The NBR did not acquire any of the LS & T ships but purchased *Dundee*, a forty-five-year-old former Tay ferry, which the Tay Steamboat Company had been using on excursions. Despite her age, she was in excellent condition, having been reboilered in 1914 and was certified to carry 997 passengers, 3 motor lorries and 2 motorcars (or 10 motorcars), with a maximum unit load of 5 tons. When loaded she drew 4ft 6in, rather more than her predecessors, and at spring tides the service could not be given for $2\frac{1}{2}$ hours on either side of low water, due to lack of water at Hawes Pier. The Town Pier at North Queensferry was also unsuitable and on *Dundee*'s arrival, the service was transferred to the Railway Pier, to which the Admiralty had built an access road.

Fares were increased on both railway ferries for the first time in over sixty years. This caused a public outcry, particularly over Queensferry which was regaining importance with the increase in road traffic. A public inquiry was held by the Rates Advisory Committee at Lincoln's Inn, London, on 12 July 1921 and resulted in a slight reduction in the rates for road vehicles as and from 13 August. The Queensferry ferry thereafter managed to pay its way, the net profit and traffic figures for 1921–5 being:

Year	No of road vehicles conveyed	Net profit
1921	7,395	— £3,934 (loss)
1922	11,639	£146
1923	11,906	— £30 (loss)
1924	12,609	£3,757
1925	12,684	£2,466

The revised rates were only valid for five years and in 1925 the London & North Eastern Railway Company (which had absorbed the NBR on 1 January 1923) requested Parliamentary power to continue applying them. Several petitions against this were received, mostly based on the inadequacy of the services, and to overcome this opposition the railway accepted an obligation to improve the Queensferry service by 50 per cent. This involved pier works totalling £21,835. At the Hawes, the Admiralty jetty was demolished and the pier lengthened by about 250ft to give a minimum of six feet of water at low spring tides. The end of North Queensferry Pier was also lowered to allow vehicles to be handled at low water and the approach to both piers was dredged. This reduced the maximum service gap at low springs to two hours, but in practice *Dundee* was usually able to run, though at times she had to lie across the end of Hawes Pier and was unable to load vehicles.

In his proposals for these improvements, Mr Calder, the Scottish manager, also recommended an increase in the summer working hours and the acquisition of a new shallow-draught steamer costing £20,000. He pointed out to his London superior that:

It should not be overlooked that, by improving the Ferry service, the Company will doubtless incur some indirect loss, both in Goods and Passenger Traffic by facilitating motor transport to and from the County of Fife, but this I fear, must be faced in any event.

London agreed to the extra working hours, increasing the annual working expenses by £3,692, but turned down flat the proposal for a new ship. Also rejected was an application received on 16 October 1926 for a six-month option in favour of Mr Harry Wakelin, W.S., of South Queensferry and Linlithgow, to form a company to lease the ferry.

The pier works were complete by the end of May 1927 and *Dundee*, relieved in spring by *William Muir*, did her best to handle the ever-increasing volume of traffic, but by March 1930 *The Weekly Scotsman* was again stating that 'road users deem the ferry inadequate and rival camps are venting claims for a super ferry or a road bridge'.

The Excursion Trade—1

With the rapid growth of motorcoach tours, the excursion trade never regained its previous importance. The Grangemouth and Forth Towing Company held a monopoly, and in July 1920, *Forth* was joined by *Runner*, a very similar vessel which the company had acquired in 1912 for towing work.

The service from Grangemouth was better than ever before, over thirty day, afternoon and evening cruises being given in 1920. This was its maximum and from 1921 the number was reduced to about twenty, though these were extended to include Kirkcaldy, with a call en route at Aberdour.

Leith (Victoria Jetty in 1920 and the West Pier from 1921) was now the main centre of the company's passenger carrying activities and, from 1 July 1920, there was an almost daily (Sundays excepted) programme. The ships were restricted by their Class 4 certificate but cruises landing at Aberdour (Stone Pier) and Kirkcaldy were frequent. The Forth Bridge was also a popular destination, but cruises further up the river were rare, the run to Alloa and the Windings on Thursday, 26 July 1923, being an exception. There were also evening cruises, usually round Inchkeith, and Sunday cruising was reintroduced in 1921.

By the close of the 1923 season *Forth* was worn out and in December was sold to MacLeod's of Alloa for breaking up. Her withdrawal ended an era for there were no further trips to the Windings, or calls at Charlestown or at the smaller river piers of Kincardine, Blair and Culross. *Runner* continued alone, with very few cruises from Grangemouth but an almost daily service from Leith to her usual destinations. From 1925 she became the Kirkcaldy steamer, making no calls at Aberdour but continuing the Forth Bridge cruises. Cruising the following season was curtailed by the coal strike to weekends and the Edinburgh holidays and no

84

runs were made from Grangemouth. The following spring, the Grangemouth and Forth Company obtained a proper excursion ship and *Runner*, the last tug to be used for excursions in the Forth area, was sold to MacLeod's and broken up at Alloa.

The Scottish Motor Traction Company restarted the cruises from Hawes Pier in connection with its buses from Edinburgh in 1921, having had two identical saloon motor yachts built specifically for this purpose. These were *Auld Reekie* and *Cramond Brig*, and while one performed short Forth Bridge trips round Inchgarvie, the other gave 90 minute cruises to view the bridge, Rosyth Dockyard and Blackness Castle. The latter produced disappointing results and in 1924 the SMT arranged with the Ministry of Works to open a tearoom on Inchcolm and started a service from the Hawes to the island. With an historic abbey, it was advertised as 'The Iona of the East' and this service proved quite popular. *Auld Reekie* also appeared at least once on the Burntisland ferry during *William Muir*'s overhaul. The bridge cruises ceased after the 1934 season, when *Cramond Brig* was sold to Clyde owners for service at Millport. About this time *Auld Reekie* was given a closed wheelhouse and remained on the Inchcolm cruises until the outbreak of World War II.

Another motor launch to offer cruises in the early twenties was *Barnbougle Castle*, owned by Walker Bros of Cramond. She cruised for a few seasons from 1922, from this picturesque village midway between Granton and Queensferry, giving trips of from four to five hours' duration to no specified destination. Launches also appeared at Portobello (*Lion* being the first, in 1923) for short trips round the bay, at Aberdour for runs to Inchcolm, North Berwick for the Bass Rock and Fidra, and at Anstruther for coastal cruises and May Island. A number of vessels have served at these resorts and some cruises are still being maintained.

Sea cruises were reintroduced in 1922 on the appearance of *Conqueror*, owned by Kirk, Deas & Company of Leith. She was a powerful twin-funnelled tug, previously used for excursions from various English and Channel Island ports. Proudly advertised as the ship with 'two yellow funnels' her inaugural cruise was at 7.30pm on Thursday, 6 July. There was a similar cruise on the following evening and on the Saturday she commenced her full programme of morning cruises to the bridge, Aberdour, Oxcars, Inchkeith, etc, afternoon cruises to Aberlady Bay, Largo Bay,

Bass Rock, etc, and evening cruises to the bridge, Oxcars, etc. The morning cruise frequently called at Kirkcaldy, as did the afternoon cruise on these days, to provide both a service to and a cruise from that town. Longer day cruises occasionally replaced the morning and afternoon runs and on these *Conqueror* often used the old Galloway pier at Elie, allowing time ashore. On at least one occasion she also sailed round the May Island.

Her advertised amenities included music, dancing, ladies' saloon, refreshments and bar. The music was provided by a live band but in her second season 'wireless concerts' were substituted. She was then advertised by J. Deas, Kirk having apparently withdrawn from the partnership.

When she reappeared in 1924, *Conqueror* sported black-topped red funnels and a grey hull, and was owned by the Stanley-Butler Steamship Co Ltd of Kirkcaldy. She started late, on Saturday, 12 July, but a determined effort was made to offer something different and a point was made of landing somewhere on most cruises. Dysart was visited frequently, usually in conjunction with an Aberdour or Kirkcaldy run, and at weekends the regular cruise was via Kirkcaldy to Blackness, where arrangements had been made with the Ministry of Works to call at the Castle Pier. The pier at Elie was also still serviceable and visited occasionally.

The season's results were sufficiently encouraging for the company to lease the Aberdour Hawkcraig Pier, which was repaired and reopened for the 1925 season. *Conqueror* was sold to the Tees Towing Co Ltd and renamed *Hurworth* but the Stanley-Butler Steamship Co retained her on charter with a restricted Class 4 certificate and on 25 July 1925 announced that 'daily sailings to and from Aberdour have been arranged, and passengers can be landed and embarked at any state of the tide'. These sailings were usually given three times daily, with the late afternoon and evening runs extended to Kirkcaldy.

Hurworth was handed over to the Tees Towing Co in October 1925, and in the following spring the company acquired the attractive *Princess of Wales* on deferred payment terms from the New Medway Steam Packet Co Ltd. She maintained the Aberdour service with cruises to the bridge and round Inchcolm for the next two seasons, but had rather an unfortunate career. Her sailings were severely restricted by the coal strike in 1926 and in March 1927 she sank at her moorings in Kirkcaldy harbour. She also broke down immediately after opening the service on 4 June and was out of commission for a week. With increased competition from the Grangemouth and Forth Towing Co, the Aberdour traffic was below expectations and the company was unable to keep up its payments to the steamships' owners. The New Medway Steam Packet Co foreclosed at the end of the season and the Stanley-Butler Steamship Co went into liquidation.

The Excursion Trade—2

The purchase of the Clyde steamer *Isle of Skye* by the Grangemouth & Forth Towing Company in March 1927 came as a surprise. Though forty-one years old, the ship was in remarkably good condition and was the only purely passenger ship ever owned by that company and by far the largest excursion paddler to appear in the Forth since the days of the Galloway Company.

Isle of Skye arrived in the Forth painted in her Clyde livery—white funnel with black top—and one authority states that she cruised for a short time under this name and so painted. She was probably on charter to the LNER on the Burntisland ferry (a duty she performed annually during the ferry vessel's refit), as by the time she opened the cruise season from Leith on 5 June she had been renamed *Fair Maid* and painted in her new owner's colours. Offering 'music and dancing on board, teas and light refreshments at shore prices' *Fair Maid* gave an unadventurous but reliable programme of sailings to Aberdour (where she often had to use flory boats) and Kirkcaldy, with frequent cruises to the Forth Bridge. She was also popular for charter sailings and took the liner tendering work. Cruises were given from Grangemouth during the Falkirk Trades, the dock holiday and on occasional evenings. On these runs she sometimes visited Alloa and Bo'ness, though more often she made for her usual haunts at the bridge, Aberdour or Kirkcaldy.

In 1929 *Fair Maid*'s owner acquired the lease of the Hawkcraig Pier, allowing her to call at Aberdour regardless of tide. Her sailings included evening cruises 'round three Inches' or 'round Inchcolm' and afternoon excursions from Kirkcaldy around Inchcolm or from Leith to Blackness but the example below is typical:

Lve Leith	11.30am	2.30pm	6.30pm
„ Aberdour	12.15pm	3.15pm	7.15pm
„ Kirkcaldy	1.15pm	to Forth Bridge	8.15pm
„ Aberdour	—	4.45pm	—
Arr Leith	2.15pm	5.30pm	9.15pm

Return Fares: 2s Cabin;   1s 6d Steerage
Single Fares: 1s 3d Cabin; 1s Steerage

Following the appearance of opposition steamers in 1934 calls at Kirkcaldy were drastically pruned and sailings from Grangemouth (which had been minimal after 1931) abandoned. *Fair Maid* then concentrated her work on Aberdour and the Forth Bridge, with a large number of evening cruises. The number of public charters from Leith also increased (reminiscent of the early 1900s at Bo'ness) and, amongst others she made cruises for the IOGT to Grangemouth and Bo'ness, for NAU of Shop Assistants, the IOGT, the AOFG and the 'Co-op' to Alloa, and also evening runs to the Forth Bridge with the British Legion and round 'three Inches' with the St Ninian's club. She returned to Grangemouth on the autumn holidays in 1936/7 for day cruises to Aberdour and Kirkcaldy. These were the last sailings from that port.

Competition was provided in 1934–6 by the steamers of the Redcliffe Shipping Co Ltd of Hull, for whom George A. Morrison and Co acted as local agent. The sailings were advertised as 'Morrison's Firth of Forth cruises' and were started by *Cruising Queen* on Saturday, 9 June 1934. She sailed from the West Pier daily until the end of August, giving morning cruises to the bridge (abandoned by end July), afternoon runs which made full use of her Class 3 certificate and 'various scenic evening cruises' (with a dance orchestra). From 10 August she was joined by *Fusilier*, a veteran West Highland steamer, which was based at Granton for a very similar programme, including calls at Kirkcaldy on Wednesdays and Sundays.

The introduction of the Redcliffe ships generated interest in Forth sailings, and in February 1935, it was announced that John S. Lochhead, a Glasgow man, was promoting a new company to develop 'passenger and pleasure steam services'. This crystallised by May into a firm proposal to restart the up-river service to Stirling, for which Mr Lochhead hoped to form a private company with a capital of £5,000. Nothing more was heard of this project.

The opening advertisement of the Redcliffe Shipping Co on 3 May carried a footnote requesting readers to 'watch for details of our New Service by Twin Screw Passenger Steamer from Leith to Grangemouth, Alloa, and Stirling. Particulars later'. Nothing came of this proposal either and the pier buildings at Stirling were demolished shortly afterwards.

Over the winter the Redcliffe company had disposed of both *Cruising Queen* (better known as 'The Boozing Queen') and *Fusilier*, their place being taken by *Highland Queen*, an ungainly but commodious Humber ferry. She was larger than her predecessors, with a Class 4 certificate for 770 passengers, and a crew of twenty. She entered service on Saturday, 4 May 1935, the Leith Port holiday, making trips to the Bass Rock and to the bridge and Rosyth. She thereafter sailed daily from the West Pier at 2.30 and 7.30 (half an hour earlier on Sundays) with a special late cruise about 10pm on Saturdays which was basically an extension of the shore licensing hours (on one occasion she was berthed by only the Captain and a boy, as all the rest of the deck crew were drunk and incapable). She was advertised to various destinations, but with nowhere to call, the advertisement soon specified simply 40 miles for 2s 6d on the afternoon cruise and 25 miles for 1s 6d on the evening cruise. *Highland Queen* returned to the Humber for the winter and came north again in April 1936. In 1936 her terminus was moved to Granton, the services being much as before, except that the afternoon cruise was extended to 50 miles for a reduced price of 1s 6d and Portobello beach was frequently advertised as an evening cruise terminus.

The company was acutely aware that its greatest weakness lay in its inability to call anywhere. *Fair Maid* had the Aberdour monopoly and the other ex-Galloway piers were either demolished or in ruinous condition. The company approached North Berwick Town Council about the repair of the Platcock Rock Pier. It offered to guarantee a regular service by one or two ships and pay dues if the North Berwick Council would carry out the work. Only a minority of councillors agreed to this proposal, though it was entertained sufficiently seriously for a quotation to be obtained. The probable cost was between £900 and £1,000 but agreement could not be reached. *Highland Queen* was sold to German shipbreakers in December and was not replaced.

In 1937 interest was expressed in building a promenade pier

with entertainment pavilion at Portobello, it being felt that this, with the established Marine Gardens and new open air swimming pool, would make an attractive entertainment complex. The project was actively pursued over the next two years and on 7 July 1939 Edinburgh Town Council finally gave its approval. It was hoped to form a public company to finance the building but the project was abandoned at the outbreak of war in September 1939.

From 1937 the ageing *Fair Maid* was the Forth's only excursion steamer. Her service was terminated by the outbreak of hostilities and when she left the Hawkcraig Pier for the last time, a small crowd of locals turned out to wave goodbye. She sailed off bravely, siren blowing and her orchestra playing 'Polly-Wolly-Doodle, Fare thee well, Fare thee well.' She never returned and in 1940 went back to the Clyde for duty as decontamination vessel at the emergency port. She was broken up at Troon in 1945.

Car Ferries at Queensferry

The Queensferry Passage, conveniently situated on the main north road, eclipsed the Burntisland crossing when road traffic increased in the 1920s and 1930s. One day, while waiting for *Dundee*, Sir Maurice Denny of William Denny & Bros, Dumbarton, thought what a boon a frequent, modern car ferry service would be. He approached the LNER with such a proposal but the railway was reluctant to invest in something likely to take traffic away from the bridge. However, it made the counter proposal that if he provided the ships, the LNER would lease the ferry to him. Denny accepted and took over the Passage as and from 1 March 1934, in the midst of growing demands for a road bridge.

Two new ferries were built, *Queen Margaret* and *Robert the Bruce*, and launched on 25 January 1934. In general concept they resembled the old Burntisland train ferries, being double-ended, with an open deck and a high bridge that allowed a furniture van to pass beneath. They were however, side-loading, with a draught to suit the existing piers and a spartan passenger saloon in the after forecastle. They were designed to do 9 knots and mechanically were 'guineapigs' for a design Denny considered could have a good future. Each paddle was operated independently by a chain drive from an electric motor, and bow and stern rudders were fitted to give maximum manoeuvrability. While *Queen Margaret* had a conventional riveted hull, her sister was the first ship to be entirely electrically welded, and comparisons were made between the two to establish the economics and the performance of a welded hull. Each vessel cost approximately £22,000, and could carry 28 cars or a maximum deck load of 60 tons.

The double-ended design dispensed with the time-wasting business of turning the ship, and with its introduction a regular half hourly service was possible, with hourly runs in the early morning and late evening. Vehicle rates were reduced, the cost for a private car coming down from 10s to 4s. Denny's manager, William Latta, soon had a most efficient service running with 99·3 per cent of the crossings operating on time (the figure is the average for the period 1934–48).

At last the Forth had its super ferry, designed for the motor age. It had its moments; Latta didn't know what to do when first an elephant and then a steam roller appeared on the Hawes Pier. Another problem was whether empty coffins should be charged less than full ones. An evening paper had its request to advertise on the reverse side of the ferry tickets turned down. The proposed advertisement read 'Buy the *Edinburgh Evening News*, the paper that wants the bridge built'.

The old *Dundee* was by no means finished and was loaned to Denny, painted in his colours and registered in his name. Mostly she lay up in Burntisland dock, but early each spring appeared to maintain the half-hour service while the new ships were in turn overhauled. She also tendered to at least one liner, in 1937, being specially painted and cleaned up for the occasion. With its new boats and ever faithful standby, the Queensferry Passage coped, in peace and war, for the next fifteen years.

The End of Two Ferries

News of the withdrawal of the 'Wullie Muir' was released by the LNER in the autumn of 1936 and her replacement, the Mersey ferry *Snowdrop*, arrived in tow at Bo'ness in October after an adventurous trip, during which she broke adrift and was nearly lost off Cape Wrath. At Grangemouth her forward promenade deck was cut back to the saloon sides to give space for cars and, renamed *Thane of Fife*, she took over the Burntisland ferry on 3 March 1937.

William Muir's withdrawal was widely celebrated. The local papers waxed sentimental over her. Once she had gone, the national dailies and monthly magazines joined in a chorus of praise, the like of which has never been bestowed on any other Forth vessel. She was honoured all over Britain for her fifty-eight years service and 800,000 miles steaming (the equivalent of thirty-two times round the world). On 4 March she was taken to the shipbreakers at Charlestown, but her deck house may still be seen at Brucehaven near Limekilns, where it serves as part of the clubhouse for the local boat club.

The William Muir
For nearly three-score years she's plied
    Across the restless Firth,
And oftentimes her prow and stern
    Have echoed to our mirth,
The wind and waves have scarred her sides
    And made her insecure,
And soon the 'breakers yard' will claim,
    The sturdy *William Muir*.

We hailed her as a well-known friend,
    'The Burntisland boat';
We deemed her quite the finest type
    Of ferry-craft afloat.
We loved her cabins and her decks,
    And, whether rich or poor,
We thoroughly enjoyed a sail
    Aboard the *William Muir*.

But now her active days are past,
    She'll plough the Forth no more:
And soon the worthy *Thane of Fife*
    Will cross from shore to shore.
But those of us who aren't young
    Are really not so sure
That any other ferry-boat
    Will match the *William Muir*!

NAN I. D. MACDONALD

With the sentimentality heaped on the 'Wullie', her successor had little opportunity of becoming a popular passenger vessel. The general comment on her is 'we went once but it wasn't the same, so we never went again'. Even so, *Thane of Fife* was a fine vessel in her own right, but she did not have long to prove herself, for with Granton in use again as a minesweeping base, the ferry service was suspended as from and including Wednesday, 20 March 1940. The 'Thane' remained on the Forth on tender duties at Granton and Port Edgar and in 1946 was laid up at Bo'ness, while Parliamentary authority was obtained to abandon the Granton–Burntisland ferry. She was later moved to Alloa where she was broken up in 1947.

The first Forth road bridge, at Kincardine, was opened on 29 October, 1936, when the sailing boat ferry between Kincardine and Higginsneuk came to an end. Traffic on the Alloa ferry, where *Hope* had been fitted up with car loading ramps just a few years earlier was also affected, and McLeod's served notice terminating their lease from Whit Sunday 1937. It is understood that they did so in the hope of negotiating a reduced rent, but the Mar and Kellie estates accepted their notice. *Hope* was laid up until sold in 1940 for service on the Kessock ferry at Inverness.

A local salmon fisher, James Bremner, took over the Alloa ferry, using the thirty-five-seater motor launch *Sunbeam*, purchased from Largs on the Clyde. He maintained the service until called up for war service in December 1939 when the ferry service was allowed to lapse.

Chapter VII
The Final Fling
1946–1969

John Hall's Royal Ladies

Neither of the firms which had been operating in 1939 restarted their services after the war. The lack of pleasure sailings irked John Hall, a Kirkcaldy business man well known in the bakery trade, and towards the end of 1946 he formed a company, John Hall (Cruises) Ltd, to restart pleasure sailings.

Royal Lady, which he purchased and had refitted by Menzies of Leith, had been a patrol boat—a modern motor vessel built in 1938 for coastal excursion work from Scarborough. She was dumpy and over-funnelled (the forward funnel was a dummy) but was one of the most modern small pleasure craft afloat. On 25 April 1947 the *Evening News* featured a photograph of the forward funnel, showing it in use as a bar store. The text explained that the ship was:

> due to run her trials on Tuesday, . . . and workmen are engaged in tidying up her decks to make her ready for use. With accommodation for 500 passengers . . . her interior is now tastefully and comfortably furnished.
>
> The main lounge will accommodate an orchestra, and the floor has been suitably surfaced for dancing, while from the band rostrum, music will be relayed throughout the ship. There is also restaurant accommodation for between 40 and 50 passengers, and in the after part of the ship . . . a special ladies lounge.

The inaugural cruise was given on Thursday, 1 May, and public cruises started on the following Saturday. *Royal Lady* was based at Granton, giving a programme of afternoon and evening cruises, some of which started from Burntisland. As with the

Redcliffe ships in the 1930s, she suffered from a lack of calling places (though she occasionally visited Methil) and emphasis was laid on the carnival atmosphere on board—'join the fun—dancing to Tim Wright's band'. Fares at 7s 6d and 6s were high but, after 1 June, were reduced to 4s (5s on Wednesdays, Saturdays and Sundays) when recordings replaced Tim Wright's band.

At the end of the season *Royal Lady* was sold at a profit to the General Steam Navigation Co Ltd and on 30 October Mr Hall announced that though her operation had proved profitable, his company was going into voluntary liquidation, as he considered there was no future for pleasure cruising on the Forth. As *Crested Eagle*, the ship became well known on the Thames and, for a short while, at Brighton. In November 1957, she left for the Mediterranean and has since plied as *Imperial Eagle* between the islands of Malta and Gozo.

Hall started again, on his own on the Tay, which he said had scenery worth looking at. However, he had second thoughts, and early in 1948 purchased two ex-Admiralty motor launches, one for each river. On the Forth he revived the Inchcolm service from a base at Granton Pier. His *Royal Forth Lady*, a typical Fairmile launch of a design mass produced during the war, arrived at Granton in early May, having been equipped at Portsmouth with a 70-seat bar and 50-seat tea lounge upholstered in leatherette and moquette and lit by strip lighting, then a novelty.

Her first visit to Inchcolm was to land sheep, then with the island tearoom reopened and a guide available for the historic abbey, she opened the public service on 9 June. Calls were restricted to high water until a World War I wreck was removed. Sailings then left Granton at 11am, 2pm and thereafter every 90min until 8pm, the final trip being advertised as an evening cruise, calling at the island to collect day visitors.

Hall's Tay sailings were unsuccessful, and during the Edinburgh International Festival of Music and Drama in late August and September, *Royal Tay Lady* joined *Forth Lady* (the Royal prefix had been dropped at the request of the Lord Lyon) on the Inchcolm service. She was a very similar vessel but with a higher enclosed wheelhouse and a high level embarkation gangway and sun awnings.

One vessel was sufficient for the Inchcolm run and, for the 1949 season, the Tay ship was given a large deck saloon, renamed

Ulster Lady and sent to Belfast Lough. Unsuccessful there, she operated on the Clyde in 1950, giving short cruises from Rothesay and berthing overnight at Greenock. She returned to the Forth at the end of that season. Plans for another ship, to revive the sailings to Bass Rock and May Island, were announced in May 1949, Hall intending to purchase an ex-Admiralty craft lying at Poole for this purpose.

A New Ship for Queensferry

By the post-war period Denny's relief steamer, *Dundee*, was over seventy years old. She looked dowdy and uncared for and was barely fit to run. Pier delays were frequent as the crew hoisted hot ashes, bucket by bucket, out of the boiler room and tipped them over the side. Her progress was erratic, and on one crossing in March 1949, she narrowly missed striking the Forth Bridge when she unexpectedly carried below it. She regained her normal route to the west of the bridge, only to zig-zag under the middle span and then turn upstream again. At North Queensferry she made straight for the Town Pier and had to be reversed and manoeuvred for almost ten minutes before she was got alongside the normal slip.

Road traffic was growing, despite petrol rationing, and Denny agreed in November 1947 to build a new vessel, although a Forth Road Bridge order had been passed that year in Parliament. However, it was 4 March 1949 before this ship was launched and, with machinery temporarily unobtainable, she was not completed until the spring of 1950. Named *Mary Queen of Scots*, she was almost a repeat of the earlier vessels but was completed with geared diesel engines driving the paddles through chains, an arrangement necessitated by a shortage of electric motors but one which proved completely successful. On her delivery *Dundee* was handed back to British Railways (which had absorbed the LNER on 1 January 1948) and was broken up in 1951.

At the launching of *Mary Queen of Scots*, Sir Maurice Denny stated that there was no intention of increasing the service, and that, in the present state of the jetties, it was impossible to operate more than two ships. The new vessel simply meant there would always be two first-class ships running, instead of occasionally 'one ship and one lame duck'. Experiments proved, however, that, with one ship crossing and one at each pier, three could be employed simultaneously and, as the pier turn-round time was twice the crossing time, this also gave good utilisation of the ferries. A three-ship, twenty-minute service, was therefore implemented, and to provide overnight accommodation for the extra ferry, a refuge jetty was built at North Queensferry.

The New Burntisland Ferry

On 13 March 1949 the press announced that 'plans to revive the Granton–Burntisland ferry service, on the lines of that which operates on the Hudson River between New York and Brooklyn, are being studied by the Minister of Transport'. Coming shortly after a decision to make preliminary borings for a Forth Road Bridge the announcement was surprising. Hall, who was behind the scheme, envisaged ferries offering a return fare of 5s for motor vehicles and underlined that this was lower than the tolls proposed in 1946 for the projected road bridge (9–12hp 3s, 13–16hp 4s, over 16hp 5s). He also announced an agreement with the Dundee ferry for a 10s return fare covering both crossings and on 25 March, the project was given the go-ahead by the government. The service was to begin as soon as conversion work was completed on four ships on which Hall had an option. These were former naval landing craft and plans included the rebuilding of the forepart of the vessels to seal the bow ramps, and the provision of side-loading ramps to suit the existing ferry slips, the fitting of bilge keels and the addition of covered passenger and car accommodation.

The ships were brought to the Clyde for conversion by James Lamont & Co of Port Glasgow, but the Board of Trade refused to accept the designs without modification. Thirteen months passed before the first ferry, *Bonnie Prince Charlie* (*LCT(4)673*) ran her trials on 30 June 1950. Contrary to earlier promises, her car deck was entirely open.

With the typical square bow and stern of a landing craft, she could hardly be classed as glamorous, but she was well laid out, with space for 30–40 cars. The passenger accommodation aft was reached by a stairway from the car deck and comprised an attractive tea lounge, cocktail bar and a well-sheltered boat deck. The ship had a service speed of twelve knots and was equipped with radar, then the very latest navigational aid. Her layout was vastly superior to that of the Queensferry vessels and it looked as though the Burntisland ferry would have a promising future.

A forty-five minute service was advertised to begin on 1 August, by which time the second vessel, to be named *Marilyn Hall* was to be ready. The last two, *Queen of Fife* and *Auld Reekie* were expected to join the fleet in the autumn, when a half-hourly service would become possible. After being delayed by storms *Bonnie Prince Charlie* reached Granton on 18 July and was joined a few days later by her sister, still known as *LCT893*.

But the service did not start on 1 August. It was announced that Hall had sold his shipping interests (including the pleasure craft *Forth Lady* and *Ulster Lady*) to a new concern named Forth Ferries Ltd, registered in England with a share capital of £29,701. Sir Andrew Murray, the Lord Provost of Edinburgh, was appointed chairman of the local Board of Directors.

The JH insignia on the *Forth Lady*'s funnel was painted out, and later it became yellow, the standard colour for the fleet. There was no more news of starting the ferry, though by the year end the second vessel, now *Flora Macdonald*, and the third, now *Glenfinnan*, were berthed at Granton. *Ulster Lady* had also returned from the Clyde and the fleet was completed at the end of January by the arrival of *Eriskay*, the fourth of the car ferries.

Minor pier alterations were given as the reason for delay in the opening, which finally took place on the April holiday weekend with the four ships giving a thirty-minute service. It got off to a bad start; the weather was unfavourable, with at least a fortnight of high winds and strong currents. The crews were also inexperienced and there was strong criticism of the ships. But by the summer the ferry was operating fairly smoothly, with *Ulster Lady* acting as passenger overflow vessel at the weekends and often crossing with pedal cycles piled high on her saloon roof while *Forth Lady* maintained her established, and popular, sailings to Inchcolm.

The summer traffic was good, but in the winter receipts fell below expectations; the vessels proved unreliable in rough weather and many potential patrons were deterred from using them. The long delay in starting the service had caused a financial drain and the low winter revenue crippled the company. By the end of 1951, its liabilities extended to £272,901 (over nine times its issued capital).

On 14 October 1952 the Court of Session issued a warrant, at the instance of Granton Harbour Ltd for unpaid harbour dues and arrested *Flora Macdonald*. The warrant notice was fixed to her mast and she was not allowed to sail. As *Bonnie Prince Charlie* was out of service awaiting repairs which the company could not afford, the ferry had to be reduced to an hourly frequency. Six weeks later the company gave up its hopeless struggle and sailings were suspended after the 8pm run on Friday 12 December. A campaign to gain Government support failed, and the official notice of abandonment was published in September 1953.

Throughout 1953 the ferries lay at their berths at Granton and the excursion craft in the Old Dock at Leith. *Flora Macdonald* was briefly in service in July and August, acting as tender at Leith to the Polish liner *Batory*, a duty which *Eriskay* had performed the previous year. On 21 December, *Forth Lady* moved to Burntisland for conversion to a yacht. She was employed first on the Essex coast and later in Devon. The ferries went to Marmagoa, near Goa in Portuguese India, as ore carriers. *Flora Macdonald* and *Eriskay* left Granton under tow on 28 February 1954 but ran into bad weather and sheltered until the summer in the Humber and at Great Yarmouth respectively. Their sisters left Granton on 3 August. *Ulster Lady* was sold to Regent Diesels Ltd of Leeds but remained laid up at Leith for some time and was broken up in October 1955.

The ferry restarted during a railway strike in June 1955 was maintained by the small motor launches *Victory* and *Skylark*. This, however, was only a temporary expedient and did not outlast the strike. One more proposal to reopen the run as a car ferry attracted little support and was not pursued.

Queensferry Bonanza

With the constant increase in road traffic and the withdrawal of the Burntisland ferry, the Queensferry Passage was soon unable to handle all the traffic offered. Frustrating delays became commonplace, while interminable arguments raged over the wisdom of improving the ferry or building a bridge. The most widely voiced ferry plan was to provide floating terminals and convert the fleet to drive-through vessels but Government money was not forthcoming. Denny, having obtained county council grants for pier alterations, went ahead on his own.

Both terminals were altered to handle two ships simultaneously, the major work being at North Queensferry where an extra slip was provided by doubling the width of the landward end of the railway pier. A vehicle marshalling forecourt was also prepared and separate access and exit roads provided to the pier area. This involved the removal of a small shipbreaking yard and the demolition of what remained of the old railway buildings. At South Queensferry the west side of the Hawes Pier was resurfaced and dredged, allowing the ferry boats to use each side.

To operate a fifteen-minute service, Denny built a fourth ship, very similar to, but ten feet longer and also beamier than the existing trio. Named *Sir William Wallace*, she was launched on 2 December 1955 and entered service the following March. A fifth ship would almost certainly have followed, had not plans for the road bridge been finalised and construction started in November 1958.

Unlike her sisters, the 'Wallace' had a Class 4 certificate, allowing her to carry 320 passengers below the bridge, and in her early years, frequently acted as tender to cruising liners anchored off the Dalmeny estate. These duties were usually fitted in during the morning when the ferry traffic was relatively slack. She was also chartered on a few occasions by a police charity organisation to give river cruises for deprived and disabled children. The highlights of her career as a cruise vessel were two all-night 'Riverboat Shuffles' when she cruised up and down between Grangemouth and the Ferry. The first, in July 1956, was a society affair with

Plate 9   Edinburgh scenes: (*top*) Leith West pier in 1901 with *Lord Morton* leaving and *Edinburgh Castle* alongside; (G. E. Langmuir collection)

Plate 10   (*centre*) the *Stirling Castle* of 1884 acting as commodore ship for the Royal Forth Yacht Club's 1895 regatta at Granton; (Mrs M. Sclater collection)

Plate 11   (*below*) the Galloway fleet at its winter moorings in Royston Quarry, Granton, 1897. From left to right are the *Lord Aberdour*, *Tantallon Castle*, *Wemyss Castle*, *Lord Morton*, *Stirling Castle* and the *Edinburgh Castle* (Balmain collection)

Plate 12 North Queensferry with the *Woolwich* at the town pier in 1908
Plate 13 Hawes pier, South Queensferry in 1963 with the *Robert the Bruce, The Second Snark,* and behind the pier, the *Sir William Wallace*

admission by invitation and a bottle of champagne. The second, on 30 April 1957, was organised as part of the Edinburgh University Students' Charity Appeal programme and attracted about 500 dancers. For these occasions the 'Wallace' was fitted with a tent awning over the aft part of the car deck, and decorated with fairy lights.

The 'Wallace' was usually to be found on the ferry. Mechanically she was a duplicate of *Mary Queen of Scots*, but being a larger ship, was slower. With her increased capacity she took longer to load and unload, and, with rather 'slab sided' lines, she could be very stubborn to move off a slip in a strong tide or wind. These factors combined to make her schedule slower than the other vessels, and as she had to maintain her station in the four-ship service, the others occasionally had to slow down or stop to allow the 'Wallace' to catch up.

Because of her length, her car ramps were placed further forward to give the ship sufficient water at the Hawes Pier. The other ships could accommodate two rows of cars forward of the ramp while the 'Wallace' could only take one, plus a row across the deck. If this cross line was tightly packed it could only be unloaded at the side at which the vehicles had been driven on. Her master remembers his acute embarrassment on an early run, when after berthing at the west side of Hawes, he was unable to unload the forepart of the ship and had to sail round to the other side of the pier to get the cars off.

A relief master found that the answer to this problem was to lower the seaward ramp and delicately manoeuvre the end car on to it, giving the others room to get off. Tragically, in 1957 a fifty-nine-year-old driver misunderstood this instruction and not realising what he was doing, reversed his car straight into the sea. Both he and his wife were drowned. The practice of lowering the sea ramp was immediately stopped and henceforth *Sir William Wallace* was loaded to capacity only when it was certain she was going to berth at the east side of Hawes Pier.

The 'Wallace's' tender and cruise duties were stopped when the continuing increase in traffic demanded the full capacity of the ferries. Working under considerable strain, some incidents were inevitable and in February 1958 passengers had to be rowed ashore in small boats after a ferry broke down. On another occasion *Robert the Bruce* hit the Hawes Pier so hard that she had to be beached at the car park wall while welding repairs were carried out. Tide and wind could also cause havoc and in February 1961, *Queen Margaret* came off second best in a collision with the Forth Bridge. *Mary Queen of Scots*' skipper is also on record as stating that on one occasion, after having stopped for a ship coming upriver, he could not beat the tide and eventually dropped anchor for the night off Blackness. Such incidents were rare considering the volume of traffic. By the 1960s, long queues of cars were commonplace on both sides of the river and the four ships were annually carrying over two million passengers and 900,000 vehicles.

The construction of the road bridge inevitably brought an influx of visitors to South Queensferry and Captain R. A. Mason, who had succeeded W. Latta as ferry manager, suggested restarting excursions from the Hawes Pier. Denny's shipyard at Dumbarton was quiet, so, in the summer of 1960, its tug/tender *The Second Snark*, was brought through the Forth & Clyde canal and restarted the bridge cruises.

She was a comfortable little vessel with two small saloons, a bar and certificates for 128 passengers upriver or 105 downstream. Girl students employed as deckhands looked very smart in blue denims and white tee-shirts bearing the ship's name and Denny's elephant crest.

The cruises were a great success and, though the 'Snark' returned to Dumbarton in the winter, she reappeared at Queensferry for the rest of the ferry's period of operation. In 1961 her cruises were extended to include a short call at Inchcolm and, two years later, arrangements were made with Edinburgh Corporation to operate a morning cruise from Granton as part of a City Coach Tour.

Denny's shipbuilding business went into liquidation in August 1963, but this had no effect on the ferry service, which was operated by the liquidator until the opening of the Forth Road Bridge on 4 September 1964. The ferry finished that night, the last crossing being made by *Robert the Bruce* at 7.45pm from the Hawes. Two days later *Queen Margaret* made a symbolic last run with 500 passengers on board, a religious service being held during the crossing in remembrance of the pious Queen, who had started the ferry eight centuries earlier. This run is now repeated on 4 September each year by a local small boat.

The four ferries were transferred to the Caledonian Steam Packet Company (as agent for the British Railways Board) under the terms of the ferry lease, and on 6 September were laid up in Burntisland dock. No employment could be found for the oldest three and they were sold to local ship breakers, *Queen Margaret* and *Mary Queen of Scots* going to Inverkeithing in March 1965. In April *Robert the Bruce* went to Bo'ness, while *Sir William Wallace* was sold to a Southampton shipyard, arriving there on 4 May. She left for Holland ten weeks later, to become a cargo carrier on the Islemeer, later becoming Swiss-owned, but still under her original name. She was broken up at Ghent in March 1970.

The Second Snark returned to Dumbarton, but in November 1963 was purchased by the Edinburgh marine engineering firm of Brown Brothers & Co Ltd, and returned to the Forth (via the Caledonian Canal) in January 1964. This firm was then engaged on a research programme for tank-type ship stabilizers and the 'Snark', based at Cockenzie, was fitted with a variety of tanks both on and below decks. Trials were conducted throughout the winter both in the harbour and at sea, but this gear was removed in spring and the ship prepared for cruise work.

She was based at Granton for morning and afternoon cruises to Inchcolm, in connection with Edinburgh Corporation coach tours. These were followed by a cruise to Queensferry (return by bus) and two short evening cruises from the Hawes, but the Queensferry traffic proved disappointing and by mid-summer operations were confined to Granton and included an evening cruise to view the two Forth bridges.

In the autumn, *The Second Snark* returned to Cockenzie to continue the research programme. It was intended to resume the cruises in 1965 but that spring, the research work was at a critical point and the excursions were cancelled at the last moment to allow it to continue.

Two attempts were made during the sixties to reintroduce sea excursions but both failed through lack of finance. In 1965 the Forth Shipping Co tried to raise capital to purchase the Danish vessel *Sunpilen* (784 GT), intending to operate summer excursions in the area between Broughty Ferry and Berwick, mainly for booked parties, and for use as a floating restaurant at Leith in winter. Late in 1966 River Cruises (Scotland) Ltd first considered purchasing the Tay ferry *Scotscraig* and converting her for pleasure work, then the Bristol Channel paddle steamer *Cardiff Queen*, which was for sale at £30,000. A share subscription was issued but less than £1,000 was received.

With the completion of Brown Brothers' research programme *The Second Snark* was restored to cruising condition. At 11.35am on 29 May 1969, she slipped out of Cockenzie harbour, almost unnoticed and returned to the Clyde, from which the first steamer had come, 156 years earlier. Her departure brought to a close the story of the Forth steamers.

Chapter VIII
Forth Occasions

Fleet Visits

For many years before the building of Rosyth naval dockyard, steamer passengers were familiar with the guardship stationed off North Queensferry and the cadet training ship *Caledonia*, which lay off Port Edgar till about 1906. She was an old 'wooden wall', with gun ports painted black and white. Various warships did a stint as guardship, HMS *Pembroke* being mentioned in the 1850s, followed by *Trafalgar*, *Edinburgh* and *Repulse* while *Favourite*, *Lord Warden* and *Devastation* were well known in the seventies and eighties. In later years the *Galatea*, *Edinburgh*, *Rodney*, *Sappho* and *Niger* were in turn familiar sights from the decks of the Aberdour to Queensferry and the Queensferry Passage steamers.

It was not always so; for almost half a century after the Napoleonic wars, the navy was never seen in the Forth. The announcement of the Channel fleet's visit to Edinburgh in 1860 was, therefore, greeted with great excitement.

The fleet was expected in Leith Roads on Wednesday, 6 June, and from that day the 11am Aberdour Passage was suspended and an hourly cruise round the fleet advertised. All day spectators lined the East and West Piers, but it was 8pm on Thursday before a solitary gunboat anchored off Newhaven. The tug *Energy* promptly went to meet her, bringing back the news that the fleet was off Dunbar, under sail and with no steam up. HMS *Edgar* reached Newhaven at 6am on the Friday and all morning *Pilot*, *Energy* and *Stokers* sailed round her with excursionists. At 1pm HMS *Royal Albert* appeared off Inchkeith, followed by the rest of the squadron, but to the crowd's great disappointment, kept well clear and sailed up to anchor at St Margaret's Hope. HMS *Edgar* and *Flying Fish* soon left Newhaven to join them.

On the Saturday and Sunday the tugs *Pilot, Energy, Alma* and *Stokers* gave cruises from Leith, while the railway company's *Express* and *Forth* cruised from Granton and *Star* came from Dundee, sailing from Leith to the fleet at 12 noon and 2pm. All the ships were packed.

Up to this point the cruises were *round* the fleet but on Monday afternoon one of the tug masters mustered up enough courage to come alongside one of the 'wooden walls' and was amazed to find his passengers welcomed on board. The news spread through Leith, Edinburgh and the Forth ports, and crowds flocked to view the wonders of Her Majesty's Royal Navy.

On Tuesday, 12 June, John Davidson & Co, Leith Shipbrokers and Auctioneers, announced trips to the fleet by *Fury, Walker* and *Tyne,* 'specially engaged from England for the accommodation of the public during the stay of the fleet'. By the end of the week many other sailings had been cancelled and fleet excursions were available from Leith, Newhaven, Chain Pier, Granton, Kirkcaldy, Alloa and the New Halls Pier, South Queensferry.

During the following week momentum built up towards the Regatta on the Wednesday and Thursday. More tugs arrived from the Tyne, Aberdeen and Dundee. Even the Moray Firth ferry came to the Forth and the sailings to Rotterdam and Caithness were abandoned for lack of vessels. The only local service still operating was the sailing to Stirling which passed en route through the anchored fleet.

The Scotsman stated it was:

a unique opportunity to view the wooden walls (but that) demand for steamers is greater than the supply. It must be admitted that some of the boats which have been pressed into service are not by any means remarkable for their beauty and cleanliness of appearance or for their sailing qualities, although their owners style them 'first class' steamers. Still, any description of vessel that presents itself at the pier is immediately crowded from stem to stern with well dressed passengers.

By Regatta day over forty excursion steamers were available (see Appendix), and that day's paper carried an impressively long list of advertisements, culminating with:

FOR HIRE, a splendid, SIX-OARED GIG 25 feet long.
For terms apply to Mr. E. Chalmers,
Publican, 20 Commercial Place, Leith.

Everything that would float was in use. In its review of the Regatta *The Scotsman* said:

> The merchantile shipping displayed a fair amount of bunting . . . and of curiously constructed items did this merchantile, or rather pleasuring fleet consist. There were smart Clyde built steamers, and screw lighters with comical little gas pipes of funnels, and crawling about a knot and a half an hour. . . . Whatever the difference of the craft . . . they were crammed with faces until they looked like pottles of strawberries.

On Saturday, 23 June, the fleet departed and the excursion vessels organised a mass Convoy Excursion to the Bass Rock. In the event, only the Dundee steamer *Star*, and *Dundalk* the Inverness boat made the distance. The fleet, 'a magnificent sight with every inch of canvas stretched before a favouring wind' sailed so fast that the rest of the motley flotilla were left behind before they had even cleared Leith Roads. The imported vessels soon returned to their home waters but *Cygnet*, before leaving, made three 'Working Mens' Pleasure Trips' to the Bass Rock, and *Stella* three excursions via Kirkcaldy to the Bass Rock and Canty Bay.

On a short fleet visit in June 1861, the combined resources of the Leith tugs, *Alma*, *Blue Bonnet*, *Contest*, *Alliance*, *Tartar*, *Goliah*, *Stokers* and *Energy*, plus the railway ferries from Granton, proved sufficient to handle the crowds, but on a similar visit on 30 July 1863 during the Edinburgh holidays, the hectic crowd scenes of 1860 were repeated. Tugs from Aberdeen, Dundee and the Tyne again turned up and were supplemented by the Inverness and Caithness mail boats. At the weekends, 4,500 passengers per hour sailed from Leith alone, and trips were also available from Kirkcaldy, Granton and Queensferry. There were more visitors than the fleet could cope with:

> The large ocean going vessel *Dundalk*, which sailed from Granton at 3 o'clock, after sailing round the fleet five or six times in the hope of landing passengers . . . returned to harbour, the Captain having made fruitless attempts to fulfil his contract.

The steamboat owners, landing their passengers wherever they could find room for them, did not necessarily return to the same warship on their next trip out and this lack of organisation brought scathing comment:

Parties have to choose between the dilemma of paying a double fare or being left on the ships all night . . . a large party were detained on board *Warrior* until 2 o'clock yesterday morning, until brought back by a steamer that went out to the fleet with some officers.

On future visits, the Admiralty insisted that the excursion ships remained alongside to take their passengers back. The normal shipping based on the Forth coped with future visits, with the home trade vessels assisting until the excursion fleet developed. The last deep sea ship to assist was the North of Scotland company's *St Nicholas*, with a cruise from Albert Dock Jetty on 26 July 1881. The railway ferries provided connection with trains to Port Edgar, *Thane of Fife* being the ship usually employed; and

Thane of Fife at Port Edgar with the Forth Bridge under construction, 1889

in later years the Wilson tugs and SMT launches did good business from the Hawes Pier. Fleet cruising ended with trips given by *Royal Lady* to view the NATO fleet in June 1947.

State Occasions

The Forth steamers were used by, or involved with royalty on a number of occasions. The earliest was on 14 August 1822, when the royal yacht, *Royal George,* carrying King George IV was towed up the Forth by the London steamer *James Watt* and Henry Bell's second *Comet,* which Bell had brought round specially from the west coast. *Comet* detached off Inchkeith, and *James Watt* brought the yacht into Leith Roads. His Majesty had been preceded to Leith by the royal squadron, whose arrival generated sufficient interest for *Lady of the Lake* to make a cruise down firth from Newhaven and thereafter escort the squadron up the Forth. Tickets were priced at one guinea each.

The young Queen Victoria on her first Scottish visit on 31 August 1842 was met off Berwick-on-Tweed by the steamer *Modern Athens,* on a day cruise from Dundee, and shortly afterwards by the GSN vessels *Monarch* and *Trident* which had sailed from Granton. Further up firth they were joined by *Albert,* with excursionists from Alloa, and *Benledi* and the small steamer *Waterwitch* 'engaged by a few gentlemen for the gratification of their Lady Friends'. As it became dark, the royal yacht was brilliantly lighted up and occasionally splendid rockets shot far into the air. The squadron reached Inchkeith at 1am where the royal yacht anchored and the excursion ships returned home.

Queen Victoria landed the following morning and two days later set off on her grand tour of Scotland. She crossed the Forth at Queensferry, *Monarch* giving a cruise from Granton to view her progress. At Queensferry the deck of the ferry *William Adam* was covered with crimson cloth, a carpet of which, 4ft wide, was also laid along Newhalls Pier. As there was no water at the pier the royal progress was halted at the top of Hawes Brae until the tide came in but:

at 11am the *William Adam* lay alongside the end of the pier. Only the Queen, Prince Albert, and the Duchess of Norfolk entered the steamboat. Sir Robert Peel, Lords Liverpool, Aberdeen, Hopetoun and Rosebery followed in the *Waterwitch*, a small steamer, which also acted as a tug for the Queen's carriages, which filled one of the sailing boats of the Passage.

To give time for the carriages to be unloaded the Queen cruised for an hour, sailing up to Hopetoun then round Inchgarvie.

By 13 September, Her Majesty was at Stirling, and *Albert* and *Victoria* sailed from Granton at 5.30 and 7am, with tourists eager to catch a glimpse of her. Two days later she boarded the GSN vessel *Trident* at Granton, having elected to return to London by steamer, rather than repeat her undignified progress north, where her yacht had had to be towed by two steam tugs for much of the journey.

Her Majesty was back two years later, this time landing at Dundee on 9 September 1844. A special cruise was organised for her departure on 1 October, *Windsor Castle* sailing from Granton at 7am with 200 on board, to cruise round and round Her Majesty's new steam yacht after her embarkation at Dundee.

On leaving the Tay, *Windsor Castle* was left far behind, and as the fleet stood well out to sea, Greig, the master, kept close inshore, hoping to head off the warships at the entrance to the Forth. Keeping his eye on the royal squadron, the master allowed his ship to collide with the Carr Rock beacon. He kept on course but, finding that the ship was sinking, he turned towards land and grounded with her boiler room flooded, two miles east of Crail. *Windsor Castle* had only one boat, capable of holding six persons, and one oar, but three fishing boats came on the scene and assisted with the rescue. Holes made in the hull by the anchor being driven through the bow were patched up but when the tide came in the vessel rolled on to the rocks where she broke up.

On 25 July 1881, after the Duke of Edinburgh had opened the dock at Leith named in his honour, *Carrick Castle* collided in the lock with the London steamer *Iona*, removing the latter's bowsprit and bringing down her own topmast. A month later, on 25 August, Queen Victoria held the massed Volunteer Review in Holyrood Park, Edinburgh, which has become known as the 'Wet Review', because of the rainstorm which accompanied the event. That evening sodden spectators were returned to Kirkcaldy on *Livingstone*, Aberdour on *Lord Aberdour*, and Bo'ness on *Fiery*

Cross, while the Burntisland ferry transported the bedraggled troops homeward. At Burntisland *Leviathan* was holed after hitting the ferry pier and sank, completely blocking the pier fairway, and causing delays to the service. She was not seriously damaged and was soon raised and back in service.

Their Highnesses TIM the Czar and Czarina of Russia arrived in the Forth on 22 September 1896, in their yacht *Standart*, accompanied by the yacht *Pole Star*. The Russian and British fleets had arrived on Saturday 19th and over the weekend the Galloway fleet and the Grangemouth tugs *Jupiter* and *Forth* were busily engaged on fleet visits. On the Tuesday morning Galloway's *Lord Morton* and *Stirling Castle* ($3\frac{1}{2}$ hours, 3s) and the Dundee tugs *Commodore* and *Renown* (1s 6d), cruised down firth to escort the yachts in. At 11 o'clock *Tantallon Castle* (flying the royal standard and decorated with bunting and with the upper saloon deck laid with rich rugs and carpets), left the Victoria Wharf, Leith, carrying the Prince of Wales out to the yacht, followed by *Edinburgh Castle*, chartered to take off servants and luggage. 'Tantallon' was expected to serve lunch for the royal party and cruise to the Forth Bridge, but the trip was cancelled because of the rain. Instead, she returned to Leith empty, going back out to the *Standart* after lunch and returning to Leith with the Czar, the Grand Duchess Olga (ten months old) and the Prince of Wales. On this occasion she flew the Russian Imperial standard.

On the opening of the Forth Road Bridge on 4 September 1964, Queen Elizabeth II crossed on board *Queen Margaret*, which flew the royal standard from a stump mast erected for the occasion on top of the wheelhouse.

A Live Bombardment

It is almost unknown for excursion steamers to carry passengers to view a live naval battle, and in this respect the bombardment of Inchkeith is possibly unique. The army erected a series of defence fortifications in the Forth in the late 1870s and in 1884, the War Office took the unusual decision to test their effectiveness by carrying out a live bombardment of the positions on Inchkeith.

HMS *Sultan* arrived off Leith on 1 August and for a week the steamers cruised round, while preparations were made for the bombardment on 7, 9 and 11 August. The tugs *Blue Bonnet* and *Robert Stephenson* were chartered to carry military observers, who went ashore between salvoes to see the effectiveness of the firing. Edinburgh's Lord Provost and magistrates witnessed the first display from *Fiery Cross*, while *Carrick Castle* and *Lord Morton* cruised nearby, so laden with trippers that some alarm was expressed about their safety. On the 9th, when fog cancelled the bombardment, *Lord Morton* had few passengers and on the final day, when *Sultan* fired her heaviest guns the noise was such that relatively few passengers patronised *Carrick Castle* or *Stirling Castle*. The defences were stated to have withstood the (one-sided) battle satisfactorily, though the gunnery was accurate and much damage resulted.

Whales

In July 1859, the Aberdour Passage steamer was diverted to give its passengers a view of a large whale which was lying stranded on the Fife shore. But the most celebrated whale came ashore at Longniddry during a gale on 2 November 1869. Eighty-two feet long, it was killed by bullets. The NBR turned the carcase into a tourist attraction, running special trains daily to Longniddry, at low tide. These proved popular, the train on Monday the 8th consisting of 40 carriages carrying 1,200 visitors. The smell eventually deterred sightseers and on the 11th the whale was auctioned under instructions from the receiver of wrecks at Fisherrow. The auctioneer stood on top of the animal and knocked it down for £120 to John Tait, an oil merchant at Kirkcaldy.

In appreciation of the income it had provided, the NBR agreed to help remove the carcase free of charge and, on the 15th the Burntisland ferry *Express*, accompanied by a tug, appeared off Longniddry. With a rope fastened to its tail, the whale slid smoothly off the beach, and *Express* set off for Kirkcaldy with surely the most curious cargo she had ever handled.

Swimming

At Portobello there were bathing tents on the sands; and for ladies, wheeled horse-drawn boxes which were pulled into the water, allowing the bather to emerge and quickly submerge, Victorian style.

The swimming club was a flourishing one, and each year during the holidays in the seventies and early eighties, organised a public charter sailing. This was taken at various times by *Lord Aberdour*, *Lord Elgin* and *Carrick Castle* but the route was invariably the same:

Charter by the Forth Swimming Club and Humane Society. Lve Leith (West Pier) 11am, Portobello 11.30, round the Bass Rock and landing at Inchcolm.—1/6 (Ladies are especially invited).

Swimming across the Forth became common in the twentieth century with Ned Barry, a Portobello schoolmaster, giving annual displays over many years, but the first attempt, in 1889, caused great excitement. On Thursday, 1 August, 'a saloon steamer' was advertised to leave Leith at 3pm, Portobello 3.45, to see the well-known Belgian, Professor Albert, swim the firth. The Professor started off with gusto watched by the crowds on the steamer and pier, but once the vessel returned to Leith, he hung on to his accompanying launch and came out of the water when only half way to Inchkeith. Unaware of this, *Lord Aberdour* sailed from Leith at 6.15pm to see the finish of the swim and off Portobello had the excitement of rescuing two yachtsmen whose boats had capsized. Then the Professor's launch came alongside and, unabashed, he stepped on board the excursion ship, apologising for his failure to complete the swim.

Lay-up Berths

The Stirling Company's boats presumably lay at Alloa in winter (though this is unconfirmed). When *Lord Aberdour* first appeared she spent the winter in the docks at Leith. Other vessels joined her there during the eighties, when the fleet expanded considerably, but by the end of the decade, Leith had become too congested to handle these craft.

The opening of the Forth Bridge so improved communication with Fife that for the winter of 1890–1 the Galloway company experimented by laying up two steamers at Inverkeithing, but by the following winter Thomas Aitken had made arrangements with the Duke of Buccleuch for the use of Granton quarry (west of Granton, near the present-day Gipsy Brae) and this became the fleet's winter base until it was filled in. It was an ideal mooring, conveniently near to Leith and completely sheltered, although access was tricky. Aberdour bay was used in the winter of 1898-9, when the steamers were laid up on the mud behind the stone pier, but proved unpopular with the crews, who objected to travelling daily from Leith. From 1899 Port Edgar became Galloway's base, and in July 1900 a small storehouse and workshop were erected near the middle pier, where the steamers lay each winter. It continued in use until the Admiralty requisitioned the harbour in 1916 and the remaining ships were removed to Bo'ness.

In the post-war years both Kirk, Deas and the Stanley Butler Steamship Co used Kirkcaldy harbour as a winter base, while *Fair Maid* naturally gravitated to Grangemouth, her owner's headquarters. The SMT launches used Leith and it was here also that 'Forth' and the 'Ulster Ladies' spent their off-duty time in the 1950s.

In pre-Forth Bridge days the spare railway ferry boats lay in Burntisland harbour, on the outside quay of the old wet dock—an inconvenient berth. A vessel wanted in an emergency might well be sitting in the mud at low tide. There was also a mooring buoy in Granton East Harbour, installed when *Leviathan* was first delivered and as a photograph taken in the eighties shows the *John Beaumont* lying there, it is possible that by that time the immediate passenger spare was kept afloat at Granton. It was to Burntisland, however, that the fleet retired when the train ferry service was withdrawn, and remained there until sold.

It is not clear where Wilson kept the spare Queensferry vessel, after acquiring *Woolwich* in 1908. Bo'ness would seem his natural choice, but photographic evidence suggests that his excursion ship, *Clutha No 6* lay, at least for a time, close to the railway pier in North Queensferry bay and the spare ferry may also have been beached there. After Denny's acquired the ferry, *Dundee* passed her long spells of idleness in the large wet dock at Burntisland, and moored to the outer quay she became a familiar sight from the windows of passing trains.

Luggage Handling

All the ferry slips, except those for the train ferry and at Port Edgar, were substantial sloping stone quays, which allowed the ferry to come alongside at any tide (provided there was water!), lower its ramps to a horizontal position, and load wheeled vehicles and animals. The handling of such traffic was straightforward, but luggage created a problem.

The Granton to Burntisland passenger boats carried the mails, heavy luggage, and much of the parcels traffic; this being brought to the pierhead stations in special vans attached to the passenger trains. It all had to be manhandled on and off the steamers and this was done using wooden sledges, which screeched like banshees as their metal runners bumped over the cobbled slipways. The sledges were horse drawn, and this traffic intermingled with the arriving and departing passengers, causing considerable congestion and confusion. It was not unknown for the horses to take fright and rear, especially after a blast from the ferry's siren, and on rare occasions a horse and luggage sledge finished up in the harbour.

South Queensferry was a particularly awkward place in the 1870s, when the railway terminated at Newhalls station. Pier and station were almost half a mile apart and the path between was steeply sloped. A team of porters was employed to convey passengers' luggage by hand. Packages which could be carried in one hand were charged at a penny; when two hands were required the charge was 2d.

The Goods Service

I used to watch the goods trains . . . when, as a wee boy, I spent two summers at Burntisland. They ran down a high hinged ramp sloping down to the deck. Across it at the land end was a big gantry having two winches worked by four men to raise it like a drawbridge, and in the midst a wee cabin for the chief-in-charge, who gave the word, seeing all. The go-on-board trains were pushed on to the hinged ramp from the rear and hauled off by a winding cable.

One day the 'captain' on the gantry had looked too often on the wine and saw, as in a vision, the mammoth vessel in place when it was not. So he signalled to the shunter afar off in the yard to shove the train on to the ramp. This done, the trucks ran violently down a steep plane into the waters of the muddy old harbour.

By bad luck I was not there to see. But later I got my first fright in seeing a fearsome diver's head . . . come slowly up. . . . There had been two vans in the train one carrying a grand piano and the other a load of sweeties. . . . A steam crane's chains rattled, and up came the grand piano pouring out floods of water and mud, while hanging down from it were long stalactites of sugar from the sweeties. . . .

The above was written in 1937 and with the following (from *Glimpses of Modern Burntisland*) captures some of the atmosphere surrounding the long vanished goods ferry:

They sailed and arrived without regard to a timetable and made little distinction between day and night . . . they provided a supplementary service . . . for those who desired a night out. Those who purposely or accidentally missed the 'last boat' from Granton had only to step across the lines there and enquire when a goods boat would be leaving. . . . The waiting time could be spent in the pier-master's bothy, by the side of a roaring fire . . . until the 'call-boy' made the startling announcement that the 'boat' was ready to sail.

The 'call-boys' . . . were lads whose primary duties were, as the name implies, to rouse sleepers to action either by day or night. . . . They were closely associated with the 'skippers' and had their place on the bridge. . . . The goods boats were double-engined, and on the bridge, there were fixed twin speaking tubes, and as the skipper promulgated the order, port or starboard, the call-boy conveyed the instructions to one engineer or the other by shouting down the respective tubes.

Plate *14* Latter-day excursion ships: *Hurworth* (ex *Conqueror*) at Aberdour
Plate *15* The *Fair Maid* on liner tendering duties at Leith Tourist Steamer terminal (F. A. Plant)

Plate 16 In the Mediterranean the former Galloway steamer *Tantallon Castle* as the *Ferah* at Istanbul

Plate 17 The post-war scene: John Hall's *Royal Forth Lady* at Inchcolm in 1948

Chapter IX

Machinery

Early Paddle Engines

The earliest ships were propelled by 'side lever' engines, the marine equivalent of the beam engine. These primitive contraptions of rods, crossheads and levers were obsolescent by the 1840s, but a derivative, the 'half side lever', survived much longer and became standard in the paddle tugs. As such, it was familiar to Forth passengers until the withdrawal of *Runner* in 1926 and survived in tugs at Methil until 1966.

It was extremely compact, with a low centre of gravity, and could handle steam at reasonable pressures. Maintenance was higher than on other designs and thermal efficiency low, but fuel was inexpensive at coal-exporting ports and for tugs its advantages far outweighed the debit factors.

The cylinder was mounted vertically on the engine bedplate aft of the paddleshaft, and the piston rod drove upwards to a crosshead running in guides. Side rods from this ran downwards to connect with the ends of the side levers, which ran along the engine base to a hinge pin at the forward end. The slide valve to admit and exhaust steam from the cylinder, was worked by a loose eccentric mounted on the paddle shaft and connected to the valve spindle by a form of hook engaging on a pin. To reverse the engine the valve spindle was disengaged and operated by a hand lever until the desired direction of rotation was obtained and the slack of the eccentric taken up. The valve was re-engaged by dropping the hook on to the pin. The hand lever was permanently connected and when the engine was running swung back and forwards in a disconcerting manner.

Measured along the side levers, the vertical motion varied from nil at the front to the full piston stroke at the rear and rods to operate the paddle shaft and auxiliaries were attached at points which gave the correct stroke. The main connecting rod was forged in the shape of an inverted 'T' with one end of each horizontal arm attached to a side lever, and the vertical arm driving the crank of the paddle shaft. For the air and circulating pumps there were scaled down repeats of the arrangement around the cylinder with side rods and a crosshead.

The steeple engine was a favourite in other waters from 1830 to 1850 but its high centre of gravity made it illsuited for work in the Forth. The only vessel definitely to have been so equipped was the pioneer train ferry *Leviathan*.

A type much more suited to the Forth was the oscillator, introduced on the Burntisland ferries, and possibly earlier on the Stirling boats. The principle could not be simpler and most toy steam engines are of this type. The cylinders swung on trunnions and their piston rods were coupled directly to the paddle shaft cranks. An adaptation of the double eccentric Stephenson link motion was fitted to reciprocate a slotted crosshead from which the valve spindles were driven.

The marine version was usually a short stroke design, to accommodate the cylinders and motion directly below the paddle shaft and achieve a low centre of gravity. This limited the maximum power output per cylinder and the marine oscillator was therefore usually a two-cylinder engine with separate rods and cranks for each cylinder. The limiting factor to the development of the design was the steam tightness of the trunnion ports which could only contain steam at moderate pressures and as boiler design improved the oscillator became obsolescent. The engines so far described were all extremely compact.

The Diagonal Engine

The diagonal which superseded the foregoing types required considerable space, and during its early development this was its major drawback. Eventually the improved thermal efficiency, and capacity for development and refinement, proved it to be vastly superior and by the early 1880s it had, in one or other of its variations, been accepted as the standard type of machinery for all paddle vessels except tugs.

In its basic form the diagonal engine was a single cylinder unit with the cylinder mounted diagonally on the engine bedplate, well aft of the paddle shaft. The drive was of the conventional railway locomotive type, with the piston rod connected to a cross-head running in guides supported by the cylinder block. The connecting rod joined this crosshead to the crank of the crankshaft. All the auxiliaries, condenser, air pump, etc, were accommodated on the bedplate in the angular space between the cylinder and the crankshaft.

This engine had the advantage of both low centre of gravity and the ability to handle steam at all reasonable pressures. The diagonal arrangement permitted a longer stroke than the oscillator and more power could be obtained from an equal volume of steam. Thermal efficiency, and therefore fuel consumption were slightly improved.

A variation which appeared on the Forth only in the *Forfarshire*, used two cylinders with separate cranks at 90°. It produced few benefits for a greatly increased installation cost, but with the introduction of compounding developed into the standard prime mover for paddle steamers. In all engines up to this point the steam had been exhausted to the condenser in a live state. It could be made to produce more power, and this was now achieved by using it twice.

The two cylinder diagonal was adapted with cylinders of different diameters (but of the same stroke) with a steam chest or receiver in between. Boiler steam was admitted by a slide valve to the smaller, or high pressure, cylinder and exhausted to the steam chest. From there it was admitted by a second valve to the larger (or low pressure) cylinder and expanded until almost completely spent, before being exhausted to the condenser.

A variation, the single crank tandem diagonal, appeared in the Grangemouth Co's *Fair Maid*. Outwardly it looked just like a basic single cylinder diagonal, and indeed it had originally been one, but during the ship's service with the Caledonian Steam Packet Co was compounded by fitting a high-pressure cylinder behind the original one, which then became the low pressure. An extended piston rod was driven simultaneously by both cylinders.

On the single diagonal, the slide valve which controlled steam admission and exhaust was worked from the crankshaft by a single loose eccentric which could take up a position either in front of or behind the crank depending on the direction of engine rotation. This position was set by a long starting lever (as on the half side lever engine) though most engines built after 1882 were also fitted with a steam reversing engine. Eccentric and reversing engine were connected to the valve spindle by cotter pins which could be withdrawn or inserted by levers operated from the control stand. To change direction the eccentric cotter was withdrawn and the reversing engine engaged. The valve was then actuated by manipulation of the reversing engine until the main engine was under way, when the eccentric was re-engaged and the reversing engine disengaged. To ensure prompt response to any bridge commands the reversing engine was used until open water was reached and *Fair Maid* travelled some distance astern out of Leith with the engineer displaying considerable dexterity at the control stand.

Dead centre was not a problem on single diagonals as cylinder pressure could be released by opening the drains, allowing the crank to fall by gravity.

It was impractical to operate a two-crank engine in this way and on such engines full valve gear was fitted to each cylinder. This was operational for both ahead and astern working and was usually of the Stephenson link type with two long eccentrics driving a quadrant of double bar or single slotted link type to which a valve spindle was connected to a link block. The position of the quadrant through the link block determined the direction of rotation of the engine. Two-crank compounds could stall on HP dead centre and an 'impulse valve' was provided to admit throttled boiler steam to the LP receiver when this occurred.

All this machinery was slow running and operated at from 30–45rpm. It was accordingly large, with each piston stroke producing considerable power. The surge as the piston passed up and down the cylinder could be felt all over the ship and, with the single cylinder engines, induced a pronounced and at times unpleasant surging motion. This was much less noticeable with the two cylinder engine and ships fitted with it were considerably more comfortable on long passages.

The manoeuvrability of the paddler accounted for its remaining in use over such a long period. The slow moving engine stopped almost instantaneously on closing the regulator, and the drag of the paddle floats and reversing of the engine stopped the ship in a very short distance. The sponsons, which on most vessels ran angularly inwards for'ard and aft of the paddle wheel, were useful fulcrums on which to pivot the ship when leaving a quay, and the way a paddler could, with a few astern revolutions, turn her bow outwards and then steam off at full speed was uncanny.

Independent Paddles

On most of the paddle steamers the main shaft lay either above, or on main deck level and there were steps over it in the engine alleyways. One of the problems encountered in designing the train ferries was to obtain a clear main deck and still accommodate the machinery. On the Tay vessels, where the crossing was fairly short, the solution lay in using very small paddle wheels and a short-stroke oscillating engine, which allowed the shaft to run under the deck. Larger wheels were considered essential for the longer Forth crossing, and each paddle had to be provided with its own machinery and boiler mounted along the side of the ship. Each unit had its own controls and wheels operating independently. This feature was useful in manoeuvring these unwieldy craft, but in running both bow and stern rudders were required to compensate for variations in engine power and speed.

Leviathan, the prototype vessel, was fitted with steeple engines, but diagonal machinery was installed on all the later ferries. To keep its width to a minimum, a novel design was used with two cylinders driving a single crank through connecting rods arranged in Λ formation. One cylinder was aft of the paddle, the other forward and the engine was contained in a small house immediately inboard of the paddlebox. Two ferries were built with this machinery working simple, but on *Midlothian*, the last and largest of the train ferries, compound diagonal engines were installed. The principle of independent propulsion of each paddle was also applied to the last generation of paddle tugs, and here the object was to increase manoeuvrability when towing. Two half side lever engines were installed side by side, each driving one paddle, with steam supplied from the one boiler to both engines. Normally, the engines ran disconnected but they could be connected when required and this was done for long runs, when the vessel was not towing. When running as one unit, flanges on the inboard end of each crankshaft were bolted together and the control levers were interlocked.

The disconnecting principle was also used in the Galloway Company's *Stirling Castle* built in 1899. Normally she was operated as a conventional compound diagonal, independent paddles only being used when increased manoeuvrability was required. The only visible differences from a conventional engine were extra control levers and a flanged and cottered joint amidships on the crankshaft. Hidden from public view were two additional spring-loaded valves on the steam receiver. One, which exhausted to atmosphere, was set about the normal HP exhaust pressure and the other, exhausting to the condenser, at the maximum acceptable LP inlet pressure.

For disconnected working the crankshaft cotter was disengaged, the boiler throttle valve to the receiver opened and the separate throttle and reversing controls for each cylinder brought into operation. The intermediate receiver, being able to receive steam from either the HP cylinder or the boiler, assured the LP cylinder of its steam supply and when the HP cylinder was working faster the ability of the receiver to exhaust to the LP cylinder, to atmosphere, or to the condenser avoided any build-up of excess pressure.

In practice, when disconnected the engine worked partly as a compound and partly as a two-cylinder simple. Its steam consumption depended on where the receiver drew the steam for the LP side but inevitably rose considerably over that for connected running. The boiler was only capable of sustaining independent working for a limited period before steam pressure dropped.

Re-engagement of the controls was straightforward but a low turning speed was probably required to unite the crankshaft without straining the cotter.

Screw Steamers

In theory, the screw propeller had considerable advantages over the paddle wheel. Its speed of rotation was much higher (100–150rpm), allowing lighter machinery at a greatly reduced installation cost. This increased speed also made for more efficient use of steam and in many cases it was used three times, in high pressure, then intermediate pressure, and finally low pressure cylinders. In such triple expansion engines the crankshaft was at the base of the engine just above the bedplate, with the cylinders directly above and a set of Stephenson link valve gear was fitted for each cylinder.

In coastal operations the disadvantages of the screw often outweighed its advantages. Screw steamers did not answer their helm as quickly as paddlers. With its higher speed the engine took considerably longer to stop and, when put astern to brake the ship's motion, the propeller initially had little effect as cavitation reduced its bite on the water until the turbulence remaining from the forward motion had subsided. It took about four times longer to stop a screw steamer than a paddler. For these reasons its use was generally confined to cargo vessels, where turn-round time at a port of call was dependent on the cargo to be handled and not on the time it took to stop and start the ship.

The first Forth passenger screw steamer was *John Beaumont*, built in 1876 for the Queensferry Passage. She was a double-ended boat with a screw at each end and power supplied by a two-cylinder simple engine. Even with a rudder at both ends, she proved so difficult to control in the fast tide flows at Queensferry that she was converted to paddle propulsion.

No further screw vessel larger than a launch appeared until 1904, when John Wilson purchased *Clutha* from the Clyde. She was also a double-ender with a screw and rudder at each end, but the vital difference from *John Beaumont* was that each screw had its own engine, a neat two-cylinder compound. This allowed the ship to be swung, using opposite rudder action and engine rotation and gave reasonable manoeuvrability.

Screw propulsion appealed to the Galloway company for the firth cruises. In the choppy water experienced at the mouth of the firth it gave a much smoother ride than the paddler, which was highly susceptible to waves choking the paddlebox and slowing down the engine. The almost silent turbine particularly appealed but it is probably fortunate that no such vessel was ever built, as the early turbines had very low astern power and this would certainly have caused trouble in the exposed conditions at Elie and North Berwick.

Galloways eventually got their screw steamer, *Roslin Castle*, in 1906. To give manoeuvrability she had twin screws, each driven

by a triple expansion engine, but even so she proved a disappointment and her awkwardness at piers cancelled out her sea-keeping
advantages. The fast-turning engines also produced high maintenance costs and her maintenance bill was more than twice that
of a paddle ship.

In fairness to twin screw propulsion, it must be recorded that
Hope, with twin compound engines, successfully maintained the
difficult Alloa ferry crossing for many years, and that in the 1930s
Thane of Fife operated satisfactorily between Granton and
Burntisland. Here the harbours were sheltered, and this was a
major factor in 'Thane's' success while *Hope* was small enough to
manhandle at piers.

Steam Pressures

The steam pressures used in the machinery described were very
low by modern standards. The early steamships operated at
between 15 and 20lb/in^2 and when the boilers were worn this was
reduced. *Nymph* in her latter days had her safety valves set at
$7\frac{1}{2}$lb/in^2.

In design, boilers progressed from the rudimentary flue type
to the haystack (vertical) which supplied the oscillators up to a
maximum of 50lb/in^2 and diagonals to about 120lb/in^2. The later
compounds and screw vessels worked at up to 120lb/in^2 and
locomotive or double-ended boilers were usually fitted in a closed
stokehold with forced draught. All the Forth steamers were coal
fired. For a full description of boiler designs readers are referred
to A. J. S. Paterson's excellent books *The Golden Years of the
Clyde Steamers* and *The Victorian Summer of the Clyde Steamers*.

Internal Combustion Engines

The petrol engine was (rather appropriately) introduced into
Forth waters by a bus company and the first passenger vessels to
use it were the SMT launches based at Queensferry. In its early
development, the internal combustion engine was limited in power
output, but within its capacity offered substantial operating
economies, somewhat offset by increased maintenance costs and

unreliability. It also ran fast; too fast to operate a propeller efficiently; and in direct drive units considerable power was lost in propeller slip and cavitation.

Electric Arc, which the SMT acquired in 1914, had been built two years earlier as an experimental craft, designed to demonstrate the efficiency of an electrical speed reduction gear between a fast running engine and a slow turning propeller. A constant speed, unidirectional, Wolseley six-cylinder engine was coupled to an alternator which supplied current to the motor coupled directly on the propeller shaft. The arrangement was designed by the firm of Mavor & Coulson in Glasgow, for whom the vessel was built. In the 1920 launches, a simpler arrangement of direct drive was installed.

The vessels built by Denny's in 1934 were designed not only to work the Queensferry Passage, but to demonstrate the most advanced technology in ferry boat propulsion. It was hoped that other orders for similar craft would follow. The advantages of independent paddles have already been stressed and the Queensferry 'twins' were an experiment at combining the advantages of the diesel engine with those of the paddle wheel. Denny's already had experience of diesel-electric propulsion in ships built for the West Highland trade and in the 'twins', two generating sets were installed amidships below the car deck. The electric motors were also below deck and the paddle shaft was chain driven. The independent paddle shafts extended to the centreline of the ship and could be coupled, allowing one motor to drive the ship in the event of a motor failure. The design was a complete success and the 1949 vessel was intended to be an exact repeat. However, with post-war shortages it proved impossible to obtain generators and electric motors, and *Mary Queen of Scots* was fitted with diesels coupled to the paddles via hydraulic couplings and chains. As in the earlier vessels, the shafts could be coupled and the ship driven by one engine in an emergency. This design proved less expensive and more efficient than the 1934 one and was repeated in *Sir William Wallace*. All four ships were entirely successful but the design was apparently too novel for conservative ship owners, and Denny's obtained no repeat business.

The conventional direct drive diesel finally appeared on the Forth in 1947 in the twin screw *Royal Lady*. Compared to a steamship, she was economical but noisy, and like *Roslin Castle* forty years earlier, manoeuvrability was acceptable but not as good as with paddles. As she was employed on sea cruises this was of little importance. Hall's later ferry vessels had twin rudders, one behind each screw, and this feature greatly improved their handling qualities.

Such then was the machinery which propelled the Forth steamers. It represents a variety of designs. One fact which stands out is the successful attempts made to overcome difficult local conditions—engines to give a clear deck for a 'drive on' train ferry, independent paddles for going through the Windings, diesel-electric chain-driven paddle ferries. The Forth will never be the same again without these craft. Few could be described as beautiful, but all were designed to do specialised work and they did it well.

Roslin Castle at Elie

Appendix I

Steamboat Liveries

Until the 1880s hulls were mostly black with pink or carmine underbody. Deckhouses and sponson houses were either black or varnished wood. Funnels were richly varied. An old print shows steamboats with funnels painted like barbers' poles, yellow or buff, and black being the most widely used colours. Red, a colour common on the West Coast, was seldom seen on the Forth. Brighter schemes were introduced in the 1880s, with the Galloway Saloon Steam Packet Company setting a trend which the railway ferries and certain other excursion operators later followed. The Forth fleets, however, remained working, rather than decorative units, and it is perhaps appropriate that their last ships were painted unrelieved black and white. The following detailed notes relate to owners' general practices, from which they often deviated in matters of detail from one season to another:

Railway Ferries (The Edinburgh & Northern; Edinburgh, Perth & Dundee; North British; and London & North Eastern Railways)
Throughout the nineteenth century these vessels were painted almost entirely in black, relieved on the passenger ships by white paddleboxes (which also were carried by *Midlothian*, 'flagship' of the goods fleet), with white beading and railings around the deck saloons. The turtle decks on *John Stirling* and *William Muir* were painted white. The goods ferry *Carrier*, which was usually on the Tay, also had white paddleboxes, but this was restricted to the facings, which had a black edging, and the covers were black.

The surviving ferry was repainted in 1902 in the colours the company had used on the Clyde and Solway since 1883 and this livery continued on subsequent ships. Funnels became red with a broad white band below the black top, the stay ring dividing the red and white portions being picked out in black. Paddleboxes, saloons, and hull remained as before with the addition of double gilt lines round the hull and sponsons, a feature which was omitted from *Thane of Fife* in 1936. The ships' underbodies were dark red, with a thin white line separating the red from the black at water level.

George Jamieson
Fiery Cross was painted as befitted her name, with a bright red hull on which her name appeared in large gilt letters. Paddle-boxes and upperworks were white. Her white funnel had a broad red band below the black top. It was one of the most colourful liveries ever seen on the Forth.

The MacGregor and Galloway, Forth River Steam Shipping Company, McLeod of Alloa, Grangemouth and Forth Towing Company, Leith Salvage and Towage Company and D. and J. Nicol Fleets
The steamers in these fleets, which together constitute a fair proportion of the area's local shipping, shared a common livery of black hull and yellow funnel with a black top. *Lord Aberdour* and the later units of the Forth River SS fleet were distinguished by white paddlebox facings, while the Grangemouth tugs *Forth* and *Runner* sported white boxes and upperworks. Other paddleboxes were black and this feature was retained by the Grangemouth company on *Fair Maid*. She, however, had two decorative gilt lines along the hull, sponsons, and paddleboxes and white upperworks, the latter also being a feature of D. and J. Nicol's vessel.

Matthew and Mathieson
While operating on the Forth, *Carrick Castle* carried the colours of her former owners, the Lochgoil Steamboat Company. Hull and paddleboxes were black with gilt ornamentation at the bow, stern, and on the paddlebox. Her funnel was red, with two thin white bands divided by a thin black band, and a black top.

Galloway Saloon Steam Packet Company
In devising a new livery for their steamers, Aitken and Galloway produced the most attractive colours ever seen on the Forth. Hulls were mauve with a dark underbody, while dark red lines were painted along the hull at deck and handrail level to form a surround for the white-faced paddlebox. The sponson houses and paddlebox covers were of a paler shade of mauve and saloons

were varnished in dark brown capped with a white beading. Lifeboats, at first varnished, were later pale mauve, and the funnel was bright navy yellow (with no black top).

On ships with full width deck saloons the hull colouring extended over the saloons and on *Edinburgh Castle* the foresaloon and sponson housings were in light varnished wood. On 'Tantallon' the light varnished foresaloon was contrasted with mauve sponson housings. About 1899 all deck cabins and saloons were repainted white, this colour also being applied to the sponson houses of the ships with full width saloons.

Redgauntlet presented a sombre contrast to the above scheme when she appeared in 1909 with a black hull, paddleboxes, saloons, and sponson houses, relieved only by a navy yellow funnel with a black top. This scheme proved so much less expensive to maintain that during 1910 the other steamers were also given black tops to their funnels, black saloons and paddlebox covers. In 1911 their hulls also became black, broken by a white line at deck level. White was retained for the paddlebox facings and *Lord Morton* retained her mauve sponson housings.

Captain Arthur
New Undaunted had a black hull with dark red underbody, brown deckhouse, white paddleboxes and upperworks and a white or pale buff funnel with a black top. *John Beaumont* is understood to have retained her NBR colours.

David Wilson and Sons
This fleet was painted with black hulls, elaborately gilded and with the vessel's name in large letters. The underbody colour (pale pink or flesh coloured) in some cases was carried up to the sponson level. Paddleboxes were white, cabins varnished brown, and funnels plain buff with no black top, except for the Queensferry Passage vessels which latterly had black tops to their funnels. On the *Woolwich* the varnished saloon was picked out in white panelling.

Kirkcaldy Towing Company
Black hull and black funnel, with a broad white band below the black top. Deck cabins and wheelhouse were varnished and paddleboxes white.

Kirk Deas & Company and the Stanley Butler Steamship Company

Hull grey, with dark red underbody. White paddleboxes and upperworks. Funnel yellow with black top. In the latter part of the 1925 season *Hurworth* ran with a black hull, broken by a white line at deck level. Funnels were red from 1924.

Redcliffe Shipping Company

Hull and full width saloons white, with a dark red underbody. Deck cabins varnished dark. Funnel in 1934 was plain yellow, from 1935 crimson with a black top. *Fusilier* was never repainted by this concern and ran in her former owner's livery of black hull with red underbody separated by a white line at water level. Black paddleboxes, white saloons and upperworks with varnished deck cabins. Crimson funnel with black top.

John Hall

Hull and upperworks white with dark underbody. Funnels in 1947 were buff, with black 'lids', followed by a broad buff top then medium width red and white bands, separated from the main colouring by a narrow red band. From 1948 the buff funnel had two narrow orange bands in the upper portion, broken by a vertical oblong within which were the letters JH with a slash through them. Oblong, letters, and slash were all in orange.

Forth Ferries Ltd

Hulls white on the excursion vessels, black on the car ferries with a broad yellow line approximately one foot from the top. Saloons and upper works white, funnel yellow. Initially *Forth Lady*'s funnel was as described for John Hall (*above*) without the letters and slash.

W. Denny and Bros Ltd

Hulls and funnels black. Forecastle, paddle enclosures and bridge white with black ladders and details. *The Second Snark*'s underbody was dark red, separated from the black by a white line at water level.

Appendix II
North British Railway

List of steamers, March 1888, and suitability for use as gunboats

Auld Reekie	9 knots	Tayport–Broughty	Not suitable for gun forward
Thane of Fife	10 knots	Tayport–Broughty Burntisland–Granton and Queensferry Passage	Not suitable for gun forward
John Beaumont	7 knots	Queensferry Passage	Not suitable for gun forward
John Stirling	12 knots	Burntisland–Granton	10 ton gun if deck stiffened
William Muir	12 knots	Burntisland–Granton	10 ton gun if deck stiffened
Leviathan	8 knots	Burntisland–Granton	10 or 20 ton gun

Height of rails above water 5ft 3in (empty), 4ft 1in (loaded)—20 wagons

Balbirnie	8 knots	Burntisland–Granton	10 or 20 ton gun

Height of rails above water 5ft 10in (empty), 4ft 8in (loaded)—28 wagons

Kinloch	8 knots	Burntisland–Granton	10 or 20 ton gun

Height of rails above water 6ft 0in (empty), 4ft 10in (loaded)—30 wagons

Midlothian	8 knots	Burntisland–Granton	10 or 20 ton gun

Height of rails above water 6ft 7in (empty), 5ft 7in (loaded)—40 wagons

(*Scottish Record Office Ref BR/NBR/8/18, reproduced by permission of the Keeper of the Records of Scotland.*)

Appendix III

Visit of the Channel Fleet, 1860

Vessels Engaged on 'View the Fleet' Excursions

Ship	Manager	Normal use
1. From DUNDEE and LEITH (WEST PIER)		
Star	J. D. Luke	Dundee–Leith & Excursions
Eagle	J. Symes, P. Duncan, P. Stuart	Dundee–Hull
Samson	Dundee, Perth & London Shipping Co	Tay tug
London	Dundee, Perth & London Shipping Co	Dundee–London
2. From PITTENWEEM and LEITH (WEST PIER)		
Forth	Anstruther & Leith SS Co	Anstruther–Leith
3. From KIRKCALDY and LEITH (WEST PIER)		
Rifleman	?	Tyne tug
Stokers	John Davidson & Co	Leith tug
4. From ALLOA and LEITH (WEST PIER)		
Scottish Maid	C. Stein, Alloa	Alloa tug
5. From LEITH (WEST PIER)		
Alma	John Davidson & Co	Leith tug
Charlotte Anne Williamson	Rogersons Star Line	Tyne ferry
Contest	John Davidson & Co	Leith tug
Cygnet	?	Tyne tug
Energy	John Davidson & Co	Leith tug
Fury	John Davidson & Co	Tyne tug

Ship	Manager	Normal use
Goliah	John Davidson & Co	Leith tug
Isle of Arran	James Johnson	Forth excursions and Moray Firth services
Ivanhoe	Cox, Macgregor & Lindsay	Leith–Rotterdam
Lion	John Davidson & Co	Leith tug
Lioness	?	?
Louise Crawshaw	Rogersons Star Line	Tyne Ferry
Olga	?	Tyne tug
Pilot	John Davidson & Co	Aberdour Passage
Prince Alfred	London & Edinburgh Shipping Co (Directors' party to Regatta)	Leith–London
Resolute	?	?
Robert Bruce	John Davidson & Co	Alloa tug
Samson	John Davidson & Co	Leith tug
Stella	?	?
Tyne	John Davidson & Co	Tyne tug
Victor	John Davidson & Co	Leith tug
Walker	John Davidson & Co	Tyne tug

6. From LEITH (WEST PIER) & NEWHAVEN (CHAIN PIER)

Blue Bonnet	Hall & Fryer	Leith tug

7. From NEWHAVEN (CHAIN PIER)

Heather Bell	Christall, Grey & Bateson	Little Ferry–Burghead (Moray Firth)

8. From LEITH (WEST PIER) and GRANTON

Adelia	A. Boyne & Co	Tyne tug
Corsair	A. Boyne & Co	Tyne tug
Night Watch	A. Boyne & Co	Tyne tug
Robert Sutherland	A. Boyne & Co	?

9. From GRANTON

Ben-My-Chree	James Johnson	Granton–Invergordon & Inverness
Dundalk	North of Scotland SP Co	Granton–Inverness
Express	Edinburgh, Perth & Dundee Railway Co	Granton–Burntisland

Forth	Edinburgh, Perth & Dundee Railway Co	Granton-Burntisland
Hercules	Dundee, Perth & London Shipping Co	Tay tug
Prince of Wales	Stirling, Alloa & Kincardine SB Co	Granton–Stirling
Sovereign	Aberdeen, Leith & Clyde Shipping Co	Granton–Wick & Scrabster

10. From SOUTH QUEENSFERRY (NEWHALLS PIER)

Thane	J. Scott, Bo'ness	?

11. From SOUTH QUEENSFERRY (SLIP OPPOSITE SPUR'S INN)

Robert Airey	?	?

Appendix IV

'Carrick Castle'

Mid-Summer Programme, 1884

JULY		Leave Leith	Leave Portobello	
Mon	7	11am	11.30am	Inchkeith and Inchcolm to Forth Bridge Works (2hr ashore)
		7pm	—	Kirkcaldy and Bass Rock
Tues	8	11am	11.30am	Elie, 1pm for May Island (2hr ashore)
Wed	9	10am	10.30am	Elie, 12 noon, Anstruther, 12.45am for Kirkcaldy. Lve Kirkcaldy 4pm, Anstruther 5.45pm, Elie, 6.30 pm
Thurs	10	9am	—	Berwick-on-Tweed. (Arr Leith 8.30pm)
Fri	11	10.30am	11am	Elie, 12.30pm; Anstruther, 1.15pm; for St Andrews
Sat	12	1.30; 3.30; & 6.45pm	—	Kirkcaldy. (Return 2.30; 4.30; & 7.45pm)
Sun	13	12 noon, 2 & 4pm	—	Aberdour. (Return 12.45; 2.45; 5.45pm)
		6.30pm	—	Forth Bridge (not landing)
Mon	14	—	—	No service
Tues	15	11am	11.30am	Round Bass to May island (2hr ashore)
Wed	16	11am	11.30am	As Monday 7th
		7pm	—	As Monday 7th
Thurs	17	10am	10.30am	Elie, 12 noon; for Dundee (sailing under bridge)
Fri	18	11am	—	Elie, 1pm; for round Bass. (Lve Elie 2.45pm)
Sat	19	11am & 1pm	—	South Queensferry and Forth Bridge. (Lve S.Q. 11.45am & 2.30pm)
		3.30pm	—	Round Bass
Sun	20	as Sunday 13th		
Mon	21	—	—	No service
Tues	22	11am	11.30am	As Tuesday 8th
Wed	23	11am	11.30am	Elie, 1pm; for St Andrews. (2hr ashore)
Thurs	24	11am	11.30am	(Kirkcaldy Races and Games.) Kirkcaldy, 12.30pm; Elie, 1.45pm; for round Bass
Fri	25	11am	—	Forth Bridge (not landing)
		1 & 3pm	—	South Queensferry. (Return at 2 & 5.30pm)

JULY		*Leave* Leith	*Leave* Portobello	
Sat	26	11am, 1 & 3pm	—	As Friday 25th
		7pm	—	Kirkcaldy
Sun	27	as Sunday 13th		Runs light to Dundee on completion of roster
Mon	28	—	—	Lve Dundee 7am for Leith. Return from Leith 5pm
Tues	29	—	—	Lve Dundee 8am for Leith. Return from Leith 5pm
Wed	30	—	—	Lve Dundee 8am for Montrose. Lve Dundee 6.30pm for Leith. (No return sailing)
Thurs	31	11am	11.30am	Round the Bass, May, and Bell Rocks
AUGUST				
Fri	1	11am	11.30am	As Tuesday, 8 July
Sat	2	11am	11.30am	(Inverkeithing Races and Games.) Land at HMS *Sultan*, Inverkeithing, and South Queensferry
		2pm	2.30pm	HMS *Sultan* (landing)
		3.15pm	—	Round Bass, calling at HMS *Sultan* on return
		7.30pm	—	Inverkeithing, return 8.15pm
Sun	3	as Sunday, 13 July		
Mon	4	11am & 2pm	11.30am & 2.30pm	HMS *Sultan* (landing)
Tues	5	11am	11.30am	Elie, 1pm; for North Berwick (1½hr ashore)
Wed	6	11am, 12.30 & 2pm	2.30pm	HMS *Sultan* (return 11.30am, 1 & 4pm)
Thurs	7	10am & 1.30pm	10.30am & 2pm	To view bombardment of Inchkeith by HMS *Sultan*
Fri	8	11am	11.30am	As Wednesday, 23 July
Sat	9	10.30am & 2pm	—	To view bombardment of Inchkeith by HMS *Sultan*
Sun	10	as Sunday, 13 July		
Mon	11	10.30am & 2pm	11am & 2.30pm	To view bombardment of Inchkeith by HMS *Sultan*
Tues	12	—	—	No service
Wed	13	12 noon	12.30pm	Elie, 2 pm; for round Bass
Thurs	14	5am	—	Alloa (light)
		11am	11.30am	From Alloa, 8am, to Inchkeith (to view fortifications), and Forth Bridge
		5pm	—	Alloa (no return sailing)
Fri	15	11am	11.30am	From Alloa 8am. To round Bass
		5pm	—	Alloa (no return sailing)
Sat	16	11am, 1 & 3pm	—	From Alloa 8am. To Inchkeith (return 12 noon, 2 & 5.15pm)
		6.40pm	—	Alloa (arr Leith 10.30pm)
Sun	17	as Sunday, 13 July		

Appendix V

The Galloway Saloon Steam Packet Co

Sailings for week ending 15 August 1897

ROSTER 1   *Lord Aberdour* (possibly taken by *Tantallon Castle* on Saturday)

	Mon–Sat				WO	Sundays		
	am	am	pm	pm	pm	am	pm	pm
Lve Leith	7.15	10.00	12.30	3.00	5.00	10.30	1.30	3.30
Lve Aberdour	8.10	10.40	1.10	3.40	5.40	11.10	2.10	4.10
Lve Queensferry	—	11.10	1.40	4.10	—	11.40	2.40	4.40
						pm		
Arr Leith	8.40	11.50	2.20	4.50	6.20	12.20	3.20	5.20

ROSTER 2   *Wemyss Castle*

	Mon–Sat				Sundays		
	am	pm	pm	pm	pm	pm	pm
Lve Leith	11.00	1.30	4.00	6.30	1.00	3.00	5.00
Lve Aberdour	11.40	2.10	4.40	7.30	1.40	3.40	5.40
	pm						
Lve Queensferry	12.10	2.40	5.10	—	2.10	4.10	6.10
Arr Leith	12.50	3.20	5.50	8.10	2.50	4.50	6.50

ROSTER 3   *Lord Morton*

	Mon–Sat		WX	Sundays		
	noon	pm	pm	noon	pm	pm
Lve Leith	12.00	2.30	5.00	12.00	2.30	4.00
	pm			pm		
Lve Aberdour	12.40	—	5.40	12.40	—	
Lve Queensferry	1.10	3.10	—	1.10	—	4.40
Lve Aberdour	—	3.45	—	—	3.10	5.10
Arr Leith	1.50	4.25	6.20	1.50	3.50	5.50

Wednesday only   Lve Leith 6pm, South Queensferry 6.40pm, North Queensferry 7.10pm for evening cruise.

Friday only   Lve Leith 7pm for evening cruise to Forth Bridge.

ROSTER 4 *Edinburgh Castle*

The up-river service timings varied to suit the tide. On four or five days per fortnight the roster is reversed and the steamer sails from Stirling in the morning. A variety of coaching tours are operated in connection with the steamer at Alloa and circle tickets are available with the North British Railway.

Intermediate calls are made at Queensferry, Charlestown, Bo'ness and Kincardine.

Monday	Lve Leith 9am for Stirling.	Return from Stirling 12.15pm, Alloa 1.30pm
Tuesday	Lve Leith 9am for Stirling.	Return from Stirling 1.30pm, Alloa 2.30pm
Wednesday	Lve Leith 10am for Stirling.	Return from Stirling 2.30pm, Alloa 3.30pm
Thursday	Lve Leith 10am for Stirling.	Return from Stirling 3pm, Alloa 4pm
Friday	Lve Leith 11am for Stirling.	Return from Stirling 3.30pm, Alloa 4.30pm
Saturday	Lve Leith 11.30am for Stirling.	Return from Stirling 4.30pm, Alloa 5.30pm
Sunday	Lve Leith 12.30pm for Alloa	

Sunday Lve Leith 12.30pm for Alloa
Lve Alloa 3.30pm for cruise to the Windings of the Forth
Lve Alloa 5.30pm, Kincardine 5.50pm, Bo'ness 6.10pm for Leith

ROSTER 5 *Stirling Castle*

Monday Spare steamer

Tuesday Lve Leith 2pm, Portobello 2.40 for cruise to Bass Rock
Lve Leith 7pm for evening cruise

Wednesday Lve Leith 9am, Portobello 9.40am, North Berwick 11am, Largo 12 noon for cruise. Return to Largo 2.30pm, North Berwick 3.30pm
Lve North Berwick 3.30pm for cruise round Fidra
Lve North Berwick 5.30pm for Portobello and Leith

Thursday Lve Leith light. Lve Portobello 9.15am, Leith 10am, Burntisland 10.30am, Kirkcaldy 11am, Methil 12 noon for Largo and Bass Rock. Return by same route

Friday Lve Leith 10am, Portobello 10.40am for Methil, Elie and North Berwick. Return direct to Leith
Lve Leith 3pm for Methil, Elie, and North Berwick. Return by same route

Saturday Lve Leith 10am for Elie, North Berwick and round Bass Rock cruise
Lve Leith 3pm for Elie, North Berwick and round Bass Rock cruise

Sunday Lve Leith 12 noon, Kirkcaldy 1pm for Bo'ness, Kincardine and Alloa. Return to Leith via Kincardine and Bo'ness
Lve Leith 5pm, Kirkcaldy 6pm, for Leith

ROSTER 6 *Tantallon Castle*

Monday — Lve Leith 10am, Portobello 10.45am for Methil, Elie and North Berwick. Return direct to Leith
Lve Leith 3pm for Methil, Elie and North Berwick. Return to Leith by same route

Tuesday — Lve Leith 10am, Portobello 10.45am for North Berwick, Elie and cruise. Return by same route

Wednesday — Lve Leith 10am for Elie and May Island. Return by same route
Lve Leith 6pm for evening cruise round Bass Rock

Thursday — Lve Leith 10am, Portobello 10.45am for North Berwick, Elie and May Island. Return by same route

Friday — Lve Leith 9.30am, Portobello 10.10am, North Berwick 11.45am for St Andrews. Return from St Andrews 4pm, North Berwick 6pm, via Portobello to Leith

Saturday — Spare steamer (probably on roster 1)

Sunday — Lve Leith 11am, Portobello 11.45, Anstruther 1.30pm for St Andrews. Lve St Andrews 4.30pm, Anstruther 5.30pm via Portobello to Leith

Appendix VI

David Wilson and Sons

Holiday Sailings from Bo'ness, 1906

Steamers: *Admiral, Royal Norman, Pero Gomez*, and *Clutha No. 6*.
Saturday, 14 July
    Lve Bo'ness   9.00am YMCA charter to Alloa (*Clutha No. 6*).
                9.00am for Leith.
                9.15am for Alloa (for Alloa Games).
Monday, 16 July
    Lve Bo'ness   9.00am for Charlestown and Leith.
                9.00am for Burntisland and Bass Rock cruise.
                9.30am for Alloa.
Tuesday, 17 July
    Lve Bo'ness   9.00am for Charlestown (for Dunfermline Races)
                     and Aberdour.
                9.30am for Alloa and 'Links o' Forth' cruise.
                10.00am for Burntisland and cruise round May
                     Island.
Wednesday, 18 July
    Lve Bo'ness   9.00am for Charlestown (for Dunfermline Highland
                     Games) and Leith.
                10.30am for Stirling (not landing).
                10.45am for Alloa.
Thursday, 19 July
    Lve Bo'ness   10.00am for Charlestown and Aberdour.
                12 noon for Stirling (not landing).
Friday, 20 July
    Lve Bo'ness   10.30am for Charlestown and Anstruther.

Fleet Lists

The following lists include all vessels believed to have sailed on passenger or ferry duties on the Forth. All known details are given for vessels which traded regularly or were owned locally. For vessels chartered, or used only on some special occasion, the entry is restricted to giving details at the time of the vessels' use on the Forth.

The following abbreviations have been used:

BHP	Brake horsepower	SCSA	Single-cycle, Single-acting
C	Compound		
CD	Compound diagonal	SD	Simple diagonal
Cyl(s)	Cylinder(s)	SDO	Simple diagonal oscillating
D	Diagonal		
Disconn	Disconnecting	SL	Side lever
HP	Horsepower (from registration book)	SO	Simple oscillating
		SS	(Single) Screw steamer
L	Lever	St	Steeple
MEV	Motor-electric (screw) vessel	NE & B	New engine and boiler
		NHP	Nominal horsepower
MV	Motor (screw) vessel	PEMV	Paddle-electric vessel
NB	New boiler	PMV	Paddle motor vessel
PS	Paddle steamer	T	Triple (expansion)
RHP	Registered horsepower	TSMV	Twin screw motor vessel
S	Simple		
SA	Single-acting	TSS	Twin screw steamer
		(1Cr)	One-crank

ERRATUM

Flying Bat and *Thane of Fife* (1936) are out of sequence and appear at the end of the lists.

Type	Name	Date Built	Shipbuilder Place of Business Engine Builder	Length Breadth Depth	Gross Tons	Engine's Horse-Power	Forth Owners and Dates	Other Career and Dates
Wood PS	ADELIA	1860	S. Shields	85ft 17ft 9ft	69	38hp	Chartered to A. Boyne & Co, for Fleet Visit 1860	Registered S. Shields To Gibraltar by 1866
Wood PS	ADELINE	1828	T. Shelton N. Shields	70ft 18ft 11ft	67	40hp	J. Morris, N. Shields 1828	On Newhaven-Newcastle service 1828 Strakers & Co, Dublin 6/1830 T. McNulty, Dublin 12/1843 F. McNulty, Dublin 12/1851 J. Ward, Dublin 8/1853 Broken up 1874
Iron PS	ADMIRAL	1876	J. T. Eltringham S. Shields T. R. Scott & Co	96.5ft 18.1ft 9.4ft	102	L. 1cyl 35inX5 1in 40nhp	J.S. & D.S. Wilson 10/9/1888-24/1/1890 Eliz. & J.S. Wilson 24/1/1890-23/9/1895 J.S. Wilson 23/9/1895-1/7/1918	Ex J. Anderson, North Shields 1876 G. Drover, Liverpool 1879 H.W. Culliford, Sunderland 1882 Inverness Trawling Co, Inverness 1884 To J. Lawson, South Shields 1918 Lost by enemy action 2/7/1918
Wood PS	ALBERT	1840	J. Reid & Co Port Glasgow R. Napier	121.6ft 19.0ft 8.0ft	92 120	80hp	Alloa, Stirling & Kincardine Steamboat Co, 24/9/1840-18/6/1858	Male Bust Figurehead To W. Hilliam, Liverpool 1858 Broken up 1863
Wood PS	ALLIANCE	1857	- N. Shields	73.3ft 15.5ft 8.6ft	56	28hp	Chartered to J. Davidson & Co, for Fleet Visits, 1861 and 1863	Owned by A. Laing & J. Westwater, Leith Remained on Forth till broken up Registry closed up 1/12/1888
Wood PS	ALMA	1854	A. Woodhouse S. Shields	81.2ft 15.2ft 8.0ft	62	40hp	D. R. MacGregor & J. Galloway 22/12/1854-6/5/1870	Broken up 1870
Wood SS	ALPHEUS	1860	- Port Glasgow	64.5ft 17.6ft 7.5ft	52	20hp	Alloa & Leith SP Co 3/9/1864-11/4/1866 David Sneddon 11/4/1866-19/9/1871	Ex Glasgow Registry To W. Sim, Glasgow 1872 J. Pile, London 1877 G. Gardner, Monkwearmouth, Durham 1877 C.H. Pile, London 1877 J. Hall, Plymouth 1878
Wood PS	ARDINCAPLE	1826	J. Lang & W. Denny Dumbarton R. Napier	97.8ft 16.7ft 9.0ft	87	45hp NB'38	- 1828-1829 General Shipping Co. 1837-1845 Tweed Steamboat Co 1845-c'1846	Ex Clyde Services On Newhaven-Newcastle service 1828-1837 On Berwick service from1837 Converted to a sailing vessel 1847
Iron PS	AULD REEKIE	1847	Miller & Ravenshill Blackwall Miller & Ravenshill	141.5ft 19.1ft 9.1ft	163	SO2cyl 34inX33in 68hp NB'55 '65, '80	B&NR 1847-1/8/1849 EP&DR 1/8/1849-1862 NBR 1862-11/11/1890	Male Bust Figurehead Saloon fitted 1856 Usually on Tay Ferry 1880-1890 To W.T. MacLennan, Glasgow 1890 OSS Piper, Port Talbot, Glamorgan 1891 Bergen, Norway 1892 Broken up 1892
Wood MV	AULD REEKIE	1920	- Sandhaven, Aberdeen	54.0ft 14.1ft 5.6ft	34	60bhp	SMT Co 8/10/1920-17/8/1942	Withdrawn on outbreak of World War II Sold to Ministry of War Transport 17/8/1942
Iron PS	BALBIRNIE	1861	S. & H. Morton & Co Leith	199.6ft 40.4ft 8.9ft	533	2-SD2cyl (1cr) 4- 44"x42" 200nhp NB'73, '87	EP&DR 1861-1862 NBR 1862-19/12/1890	Train Ferry To W.T. MacLennan, Glasgow 1890 T.C. Glover, Edinburgh 1892 Broken up 1892
- PS	BEDLINGTON						J. & M. Anderson 1851-1852	Purchased for use as train ferry on Tay crossing, but never sailed on Forth or Tay
Wood PS	BENLEDI	1837	R. Barclay, Glasgow	124ft 16ft 9ft	156		T. Barclay 1837 A. Greig 1/1838-1844 Edinburgh & Dundee SP Co 1844-1846	On Stirling service 1837 On Largo & Dundee services 1838-1846 Broken up 1846
Wood PS	BENLOMOND	1825	J. Lang Dumbarton R. Napier	90.9ft 16.0ft 8.0ft	70	1cyl 35hp NB'33	T. Barclay 1833-1836	Ex J. Lang (Benlomond Steamboat Co) 1825 A. McEarchan (West Highland services) 1828 R. Napier, Glasgow 1832 On Stirling service 1833-1835 To Flensburg SS Co, Denmark 1836 Frahm, Kiel, Germany 1841

Type	Name	Date Built	Shipbuilder Place of Business Engine Builder	Length Breadth Depth	Gross Tons	Engine's Horse-Power	Forth Owners and Dates	Other Career and Dates
Iron PS	BEN-MY-CHREE	1845	R. Napier Govan	152.2ft 23.4ft 12.5ft	256	SL2cyl 120hp	J. Johnson 10/5/1860-6/12/1861 (Used on Forth at Fleet Review 1860 and on 15/6/1861)	Ex Isle of Man SP Co 1845 To J. Mackillican, Invergordon 1861 H. E. Moss, Liverpool 1862 Stewart & Douglas, Liverpool 1862 A hulk at Bonny, Nigeria by 1915
Wood PS	BENWELL	1858	- R. Shields	67.4ft 13.0ft 7.3ft	38		John Croall 22/4/1864-2/1867 (Used on Queensferry Passage)	Ex Newcastle Registry Burnt out at North Queensferry 2/1867
Iron PS	BETEFDOE	1875	J. Readhead & Co South Shields Readhead & Co	107.3ft 19.0ft 9.7ft	131	L2cyl 29"x50 5/8" 56nhp NB'92	J.S. Wilson 6/12/1913-18/5/1915	Ex CHAMPION, T.W. Elliott, London 1875 Sold Foreign (Belgium) 1878 (France) 1880 Renamed BETEFDOE 1913 To R.C. Baister, Sunderland 1915
Wood PS	BLUE BONNET	1857	W. Thorburn North Shields J. Pulmond	83.4ft 17.2ft 9.5ft	72	L1cyl 35hp	R. Hall & H. Fraser 25/6/1857-1861 MacGregor & Galloway 1861-5/7/1864	To A. Laing & M. P. Galloway, Leith 1864 A. Laing & W. Thomson, Leith 1865 A. Laing & E. Geoff, Leith 1868 R. Gilmour, Burntisland 1888 W. Taylor, Grangemouth 1892 Forth Towing Co, Grangemouth 1892 Destroyed by fire 31/7/1892
Wood PS	(New) BLUE BONNET	1866	- N. Shields	82.6ft 17.1ft 9.1ft	75	L1cyl 34hp	MacGregor & Galloway 5/5/1870-24/1/1872 / W. Beveridge 9/4/1875-30/6/1883	Ex North Shields Registry To Galloway and Nelson, Elie 1872 Mackie and Nelson, Elie 1872 Mackie and Sneddon, Alloa 1873 Salveson and Mackie, Leith 1873 Salveson and Kennedy, Leith 1873 Beveridge and Kennedy, Alloa 1875 To Scottish Steam Fishing Co, Granton 1883 Renamed MERLIN 1883 Destroyed by fire off May Island 28/11/1884
Iron PS	BOLD BUCCLEUCH	1847	Smith & Rodger Govan	149.0ft 17.1ft 9.1ft	209		Edinburgh & Dundee SP Co, 1847-1849	Standing bowsprit, two masts To D. Harmer, Great Yarmouth 1849 Sold at Leghorn, Italy 1862
Wood PS	BONNIE DUNDEE	1837	T. Adamson Dundee P. Borrie	120.4ft 17.7ft 10.4ft	128 296		Dundee & Leith SP Co 29/3/1837-11/3/1839 G. Fyfe, Dundee 5/3/1840-9/3/1840 Aberdeen, Leith & Clyde Shipping Co 9/3/1840-3/1853	Women Bust Figurehead, three masts Held as security by Eastern Bank, Dundee 1839-1840 Lengthened by 23ft 1841 On Dundee service 1837-1839 On Aberdeen service 1840-1853 To Maryport SS Co, Maryport 1853 Broken up, Liverpool 1/1856
Steel TSMV	BONNIE PRINCE CHARLIE	1943	Stockton Construction Co, Stockton Davey, Paxman & Co (Colchester) Ltd	180.0ft 38.1ft 7.0ft	469	2 sets 4 SCSA each12cyl 7"X7¼"	Forth Ferries Ltd 1950-1954	Ex Admiralty LCT (4) 673-50 Converted by James Lamont & Co, Port Glasgow 1950 To Timblo, Irmados, Ltda, Goa, India 1954 Renamed SURENDRA 1954
Wood PS	BOREAS	1872	- Low Walker	82.4ft 16.8ft 9.3ft	66	SL 1cyl 28½"X48" 27hp	David Wilson 16/9/1876-24/1/1890 Elisabeth Wilson 24/1/1890-19/4/1898	Ex Broken up at Bo'ness Registry closed 19/4/1898
Wood PS	BRILLIANT	1821	J. Lang & Co Dumbarton	120ft 20ft 12ft	159	2cyl 80hp	Leith & Aberdeen SY Co 1821-1826 Aberdeen, Leith & Clyde Shipping Co 1826-12/12/1839	On Aberdeen service 1821-1839 Wrecked entering Aberdeen Harbour and destroyed by fire 12/12/1839

Type	Name	Date Built	Shipbuilder Place of Business Engine Builder	Length Breadth Depth	Gross Tons	Engine's Horse-Power	Forth Owners and Dates	Other Career and Dates
Iron PS	BRITANNIA	1843	Smith & Rodger Glasgow	165.5ft 21.2ft 10.0ft	207		Edinburgh & Dundee SP Co 1945-10/3/1847	Standing bowspit, three masts On Dundee service 1845-1847 To Hull & Leith SP Co 1847 Germany 1863
Iron PS	BURNTISLAND	1844	J. B. Maxton & Co Leith Second hand engines Fitted by Maxton	120ft 20ft		2X35hp	John Gladstone & the Duke of Buccleuch 1844-1/1/1847 E&NR 1/1/1847-1/8/1849 EP&DR 1/8/1849-4/1851	Engines purchased from the Oak Farm Co, near Dudley, Worcs. On Granton-Burntisland ferry 1844-1851 Used on Tay Crossing 1849 To J. Bremner, Liverpool 1851
Iron PS	CAMBRIA	1879	T. Redhead & Son Preston R. Smith	118.7ft 20.4ft 9.9ft	157	L 2cyl 31½"X48" 70rhp	Leith Salvage & Towage Co	Used for passenger charter 1922 NB'94
Iron SS	CAMEO	1867	A. McMillan & Son Dumbarton P. Taylor, Falkirk	65.9ft 16.7ft 7.1ft	60	S 1cyl 10½"X12" 16hp (made '67)	Absalom Weir, Leith 1874-20/8/1877 R. Wilson, Stirling 20/8/1877-5/4/1895	Ex J. & C. Robertson, Grangemouth 1867 R. & J. Stephenson, Middlesborough 1871 To P. Lallinan, Cork, Ireland 1895 Broken up 12/1928
Iron PS	CARHAM	1864	A. & J. Inglis Glasgow	141.8ft 20.0ft 8.5ft	158	SO 2cyl 42"X48" 60nhp	North British SP Co 1868-1869	Ex NBSP, Silloth services 1864 To NBSP, Clyde services 1869 Highland Railway, Strome Ferry 1872 Bournemouth SP Co 1882 Ramsgate Steamship Co 1883 Renamed QUEEN OF THANET 1883 R. & D. Jones, Liverpool 1889 Broken up 1889
SS	CARRADALE	1857	J. & R. Swan Glasgow Smith Brothers	80.3ft 15.0ft 6.6ft	51	S 2cyl	Peter Brash 21/9/1869-5/7/1873	Ex Glasgow Registry To St. Paul de Loanda
Iron PS	CARRICK CASTLE	1870	J. Fullarton & Co Paisley W. King & Co	192.1ft 18.2ft 7.0ft	176	D 1cyl 49"X54" 85nhp	W. Mathieson & G. Matthew 1881-3/4/1885	Ex Lochgoil Steamboat Co, Glasgow 1870 To A. Paine, Hastings 1885 Bristol Channel Passenger services, Cardiff 1889 Renamed LADY MARGARET 1889 J. Gunn, Cardiff Renamed LORD TREDEGAR 1895 P. Baker, Cardiff & Broken up 1896
Iron PS	CARRIER	1858	Scott & Co Greenock Greenock Foundry Co	124.4ft 24.7ft 8.5ft	243	SO 2cyl 42"X36" 120nhp NB'66 '73	EP&DR 1858-1862 NBR 1862-5/11/1881	Train ferry, usually on Tay ferry 1858-1878 To S.L. Mason, Edinburgh 1881 Isle of Wight Marine Transit Co 1884 LB&SCR 1887 Broken up in Sweden 1893
Wood PS	CARRS	1852	John Bell North Shields	72.5ft 13.9ft 7.0ft	54		MacGregor & Galloway 13/10/1853-16/4/1855	Ex C. Carr, Newcastle 1852 To S. Humpray, Cardiff 1855 G.T. Winther, Cowes 1867 Converted to a landing stage 1878
PS	CHARLOTTE ANNE WILLIAMSON	1860	- St. Peter's Quay	114ft 16ft 7ft	82	40hp	Used at Fleet Visit 1860	Owned by John Rogerson, Newcastle Broken up 1883
Wood PS	CITY OF EDINBURGH	1821	Wigram & Green Blackwall Boulton & Watt		135	80hp	London & Edinburgh SP Co 1821-1836	On Newhaven-London service 1821-1836 To General Steam Navigation Co 1836 Wrecked at Ostend 3/4/1842
Iron TSS	CLUTHA No. 6	1884	T. B. Seath & Co Rutherglen Clyde Nav. Trust	100.0ft 14.0ft 5.7ft	75	2 C2cyl 7"&13"X12")3nhp	J.S. Wilson 20/9/1904-13/11/1917	Ex The Clyde Nav. Trust 1884 New Engines 1901 To J.S. McGillivray, Macduff 1917
Wood PS	COMET	1812	J. Wood Port, Glasgow J. Robertson	43.5ft 11.2ft 5.6ft	24	L 1cyl 11"X16" 4hp	Henry Bell (Visited Forth 1813)	First practical steamboat in Europe New engines and lengthened by 22ft 1819 Wrecked near Craignish, Argyll 12/1820

Type	Name	Date Built	Shipbuilder Place of Business Engine Builder	Length Breadth Depth	Gross Tons	Engine's Horse-Power	Forth Owners and Dates	Other Career and Dates
Wood PS	COMET	1821	J. Lang Dumbarton D. McArthur & Co		94	24hp	Henry Bell (On Forth 1823 for visit of King George IV)	Sunk off Gourock 25/10/1825 Raised and converted to sailing vessel Broken up 1876
Wood PS	COMET	1834	- Rotherhithe, Surrey	135.8ft 16.6ft 9.0ft			E&NR 3/8/1848-1/8/1849 EP&DR 1/8/1849-26/3/1852 J. & M. Anderson 26/3/1852-c'1854	Ex Miller & Ravenshill, Blackwall 1848 Bowsprit, Woman Bust Figurehead On Granton-Burntisland Ferry 1848-1850 Usually on Tay Ferry 1850-1853 Fitted with saloon c'1851 To ?
-	COMMODORE	-	-	-	-	-	-	See GLADSTONE
Iron PS	CONQUEROR	1897	J. T. Eltringham & Co South Shields Hepple & Co	131.0ft 21.7ft 10.0ft	199	L 2cyl 31½"X58" 150nhp	Kirk Deas & Co 1922-1923 Stanley Butler SS Co 1924 (Retained on charter 1925)	Ex T. G. Sandford, Gravesend 1897 Dick & Page, London 1903 Jersey Steam Shipping Co 1920 To Tees Towing Co 1925 Renamed HURWORTH 1925 subsequently renamed HUTTON CROSS Broken up 1934
Wood PS	CONQUEST	1867	- N. Shields J. P. Almond	81.1ft 17.1ft 9.2ft	69	L 1cyl 30nhp	J. S. Wilson 31/5/1899-16/5/1914	Ex D. Sneddon, Alloa 1867 -, Dundee 1890 Broken up 1914
Wood PS	CONTEST	1856	- N. Shields	77.5ft 16.6ft 8.8ft	64	L 1cyl 30hp	Chartered to J. Davidson & Co for Fleet Visits - 1860, 1861 and 1863	Owned by Helen Stoker & George Jamieson, Leith
Wood PS	CORNUBIA	1832	J. Scott & Sons Greenock	108ft 18ft 11ft	94nt		St. George SP Co (on charter) 1838-1839	On Aberdeen-Leith service Owned by Plymouth, Falmouth & Penzance SP Co
Wood PS	CORSAIR	1852	- S. Shields	79.4ft 15.7ft 8.8ft	59	L 1cyl 36hp	A. Laing & A. Boyne Used at Fleet Visit 1860	
SS	CORSAIR	1867	- Port Glasgow	63.8ft 17.0ft 7.6ft	54	S 2cyl 18hp	J. C. Tait 30/6/1874-9/4/1878	Ex D. Cowan & Co, Glasgow 1887 To W. Ford, Edinburgh 1878 Wrecked at Stonehaven 3/1881
Wood PS	COUNTESS						Subscribers to Alloa Ferry 1830's-1845 Edinburgh & Glasgow Railway 1845-1852	Alloa Ferry steamer Sank at Alloa 7/1852
Iron PS	COUNTESS OF KELLIE	1870	A. Stephen & Sons Glasgow J. Howden & Co	81.1ft 19.1ft 6.1ft	68	D 2cyl 14"X30" 30hp	Caledonian Railway 1/1870-4/10/1887	Double bowed, no masts To D. MacBrayne, Glasgow Converted into screw driven cargo vessel J. Donaldson, Glasgow 1904 J. Skipp, Stockton 1913 Reduced to a hulk 1/1934
Wood MV	CRAMOND BRIG	1921	Sandhaven, Aberdeen	54.0ft 14.1ft 5.6ft	34	9nhp	SMT 4/2/1921-3/7/1944	Chartered to Clyde operators in 1934 and did not return to Forth. To Ministry of War Transport 1944 Cruised on Loch Ness 1958 A.A. Mackenzie, Leith 1961 J. McMillan, Campbeltown 1963 Wrecked 21/1/1966
Steel PS	CRUISING QUEEN	1903	Gourlay Brothers Dundee Gourlay Brothers	190.1ft 25.5ft 7.9ft	302	98rhp	Redcliffe Shipping Co 1934	Ex CLEETHORPES Gt. Central Railway, Hull 1903 LNER, Hull 1923 To Broken up 1934
Wood PS	CYCLOPS	1829	Glasgow		34	14hp	Forth & Clyde Canal Co 1829-?	Stern-wheeler On Glasgow-Grangemouth-Alloa service
Wood PS	CYGNET	1859	- Blackwall, Durham	70ft 14ft 7ft	43	20hp	Used at Fleet Visit 1860	Owned by J. Robson, Gateshead
Wood TSS	DALMENY CASTLE	1887	J. Arthur Dalmeny J. Arthur	46.0ft* 8.3ft 3.5ft	10	2 Eng. Inverted C, 5½"X10"X9" 7hp	John Arthur 1887-29/12/1893 J. S. Wilson 29/12/1893-26/12/1895	*As lengthened 1888 Steam Launch Broken up at Bo'ness 1895
Iron PS	DANDIE DINMONT	1866	A. & J. Inglis Glasgow A. & J. Inglis	197.2ft 22.1ft 6.9ft	215	SDO 2 cyl 40"X60" 110nhp	North British SP Co 1867-1869	From & To NBSP, Clyde services, To Southsea, Ventnor, Sandown & Shanklin SB Co 1881 Wrecked 1901

Type	Name	Date Built	Shipbuilder Place of Business Engine Builder	Length Breadth Depth	Gross Tons	Engine's Horse-Power	Forth Owners and Dates	Other Career and Dates
Wood PS	DERWENT	1860	-, Low Walker	78ft 16ft 9ft	68	30hp	Used at Fleet Visit 1863	Owned by J. Newton & R. Taylor, Aberdeen
Steel PS	DOLPHIN	1885	-, Port Glasgow	88.9ft 17.1ft 8.0ft	85	40hp	J.S. Wilson 1890-1919 Leith Salvage & Towage Co 1919-27/7/1920	Ex Sir William Arrol & Co Forth bridge construction vessel Used by Wilson on Tay Ferry Broken up 1920
Iron SS	DREDGER NO 1	1871	-, Renfrew				J.S. Wilson 26/10/1918-29/10/1919	Ex Clyde Navigation Trust To Leith Salvage & Towage Co Ltd
Steel PS	DUCHESS OF BUCCLEUCH	1915	A. & J. Inglis Glasgow A. & J. Inglis	224.5ft 28.0ft 8.4ft	450	CD 2cyl 37", 67"X66" 303nhp	Built for the Galloway Saloon SP Co but never delivered	Sold to Admiralty and completed as a minesweeper Broken up Llanelly 1921
Wood PS	DUKE OF RICHMOND	1838	J. Wood Port Glasgow		497	120hp	Aberdeen, Leith & Clyde Shipping Co 1838-1859	Lengthened by 12ft 1843 On Aberdeen service 1838-1859 Wrecked near Aberdeen 8/10/1859
Wood PS	DUMBARTON	1820	W. Denny Dumbarton D. McArthur	83.5ft 14.1ft 7.8ft	71	24hp	T. Barclay 1833-2/1834 A. Greig 2/1834-17/6/1835	Bowsplit & Female Bust Figurehead Ex Dumbarton Steamboat Co On Stirling service 1833-1834 To W. Hutton, Dundee 1835 W.B. McKean(Forth Steam Towing Co) 1836 Broken up at Leith 1852
Wood PS	DUMBARTON CASTLE	1815	A. McLachlan Dumbarton D. McArthur	87.0ft 16.5ft 7.7ft	108	2cyl 30hp	Edinburgh, Glasgow & Leith Shipping Co 9/1819-c'1824	Ex Clyde services On Grangemouth-Leith-Dysart services 1819-1824 To Sold at Dumbarton 1/6/1825
Iron PS	DUNDALK	1844	R. Napier Glasgow	179.0ft 26.1ft 15.4ft	552	2cyl 250hp	Used at Fleet Visits 1860 & 1863	Owned by the North of Scotland SP Co
Iron PS	DUNDEE	1875	W. Simons & Co Renfrew W. Simons & Co	149.3ft 27.1ft 7.1ft	264	CD 2cyl 23", 42"X42" 80rhp NB'14	NBR 16/8/1920-1/1/1923 LNER 1/1/1923-28/9/1934 W. Denny & Brothers Ltd 28/9/1934-14/8/1951	Ex Dundee Harbour Trustees 1875 Tay Steamboat Co Ltd 1917 To British Transport Commission 1951 Broken up and Registry closed 29/4/1952
Iron SS	EAGLE	1858	Gourlay Brothers Dundee	164.3ft 22.8ft 12.6ft	318	S 2cyl 85hp	Used at fleet visit 1860	Owned by P. Duncan & P. Stuart, Dundee
Wood PS	EARL OF KELLIE	1826	Sime & Rankine Leith	96.7ft 20.0ft 10.5ft	171		Fife & Midlothian Ferry Trustees 17/8/1826-5/3/1839	Bowsplit, Figurehead, two masts Newhaven-Pettycur & Kirkcaldy ferry 1826-1839 To Swan Brothers, Kirkcaldy 1839 Wrecked on coast of Sweden 21/9/1849
Iron TSS	EARL OF POWIS	1882	R. Duncan & Co Port Glasgow Rankine & Blackmore	105.6ft 21.3ft 7.6ft	116	C 2cyl 18"&34" X24" 50hp	Used for passenger charters Early 1920's	Owned by Leith Salvage & Towage Co, Leith
Iron PS	EARL OF HOSSLYN	1847	Smith & Rodger Glasgow	141.7ft 17.0ft 9.0ft	191		Edinburgh & Dundee SP Co 1847-18/6/1849	Standing Bowsprit, two masts On Dundee service 1847-1849 To Mecklenburg SP Co, Wismar 1849
Wood PS	ECLIPSE	1836	- Shields		69	39hp	Shields & Newcastle General SN Co 1839	On Hull-Leith/Dundee service Lengthened 1839
Wood PS	EDINBURGH CASTLE	1821	J. & C. Wood Port Glasgow	90.0ft 18.9ft 10.9ft	95		Fife & Midlothian Ferry Trustees 1821-29/7/1845 Kirkcaldy, Leith & Newhaven Ferry SB Co 29/7/1845-29/3/1849	Billet Head, two masts To T. Ness, Leith Engines removed 1849 Jersey SN Co, Jersey 1849 T. Rose, Jersey 1851 F.I. Graduia, Jersey 1854 Broken up 1855
Steel PS	EDINBURGH CASTLE	1886	J. Scott & Co Kinghorn & Kirkcaldy J. Scott & Co	160.0ft 20.1ft 7.0ft	158	D 1cyl 48"X60" 85nhp NB'97	Galloway Saloon SP Co 1886-12/8/1917	Requisitioned for minesweeping duties 28/6/1916 To Admiralty 1917 Converted to Hospital Carrier HC6. Blown up by British Forces in White Sea, Russia 24/9/1919

Type	Name	Date Built	Shipbuilder Place of Business Engine Builder	Length Breadth Depth	Gross Tons	Engine's Horse-Power	Forth Owners and Dates	Other Career and Dates
Wood MEV	ELECTRIC ARC	1911	MacLaren Brothers Dumbarton Mavor & Coulson	50ft 12ft 7ft		Wolseley 6cyl + electrics 45bhp	SMT Co 1914-c'1916	Ex Mavor & Coulson Ltd, Glasgow 1911 Requisitioned by Admiralty 1916 for duties at Rosyth. Burnt out near Port Edgar c'1916
Wood PS	ENERGY	1856	- S. Shore, Durham	80, 4ft 16, 4ft 8, 8ft	68	L 1cyl 30hp	MacGregor & Galloway 25/2/1857-24/7/1862	Ex E. R. Elliot, Gateshead 1856 To F. J. Leach, Middlesborough 1862 Lost 10/10/1863
Steel TSMV	ERISKAY	1943	Stockton Construction Co, Stockton Davey, Paxman (Colchester) Ltd.	180, 0ft 38, 1ft 6, 7ft	384	2 sets 4 SCSA each 12cyl 7"X7½"	Forth Ferries Ltd, 1950-1954	Ex Admiralty LCT (4) 668-50 Converted by James Lamont & Co, Port Glasgow 1950 To Timblo, Irmados, Ltda, ---- Goa, India 1954 Renamed PRADIPA 1954
Iron PS	EXPRESS	1848	Miller & Ravenshill Blackwall Miller & Ravenshill	153, 0ft 24, 1ft 9, 8ft	268 260	120nhp NB '51, '54, '63	E&NR 1/1/1849-1/8/1849 EP&DR 1/8/1849-1862 NBR 1862-7/9/1878	Full Man Figurehead Saloon fitted 1851 Broken up 1878
Steel PS	FAIR MAID	1886	S. McKnight & Co, Ayr Hutson & Corbett, Compounded 1891 Rankin & Blackmore	190, 0ft 20, 0ft 7, 1ft	211	CD(1cr) 27"X49" X60" 104nhp NB'03	Grangemouth and Forth Towing Co, 3/1927-12/1940	Ex MADGE WILDFIRE R. Campbell, Glasgow 1886 Caledonian SP Co, Gourock 1889 A. W. Cameron, Dumbarton 1911 Buchanan Steamers Ltd., Glasgow 1913 Renamed ISLE OF SKYE 1913 Williamson Buchanan Steamers Ltd 1919 To Ministry of War Transport, Glasgow 1940 Broken up at Troon 1945
Iron PS	FAIR TRADER	1848	Smith & Rodger Govan	147, 0ft 16, 2ft 7, 5ft	76		Edinburgh & Dundee SP Co 1847-26/6/50	Standing Bowsprit, two masts On Newhaven to Largo service 1847-1849 To H. P. Prior, Copenhagen 1850
Wood PS	FIERY CROSS	1867	Brodie & Maxwell Cobble Dean W. Scott	87, 3ft 18, 3ft 9, 3ft	87	L 1cyl 33"X48" 35hp	G. Jamieson 19/4/1872-17/9/1893	Ex T. A. Alderson, Newcastle 1867 J. Pie, Kirkcaldy 1870 J. G. Howison, Burntisland 1871 To C. Munro (Executor) 1893 J. Henderson, Leith 1894 W. Taylor, Grangemouth 1894 W. J. Rowe, Glasgow 1898 Broken up, Registry closed 24/1/1899
Iron PS	FIFESHIRE	1887	J. T. Eltringham South Shields J. P. Rennoldson	180, 0ft 18, 8ft 9, 8ft	132	L 1cyl 36"X54" 80nhp	Kirkcaldy Towing Co, 5/5/1905-23/4/1917	Ex Clyde Shipping Co, Glasgow 1887 Named FLYING SWALLOW J. T. Eltringham 1904 To C. Duncan & Sons, Middlesborough 1917 Leith Salvage & Towage Co, Leith 1919 Broken up 1924
Steel TSMV	FLORA MACDONALD	1943	P. & W. MacLellan Ltd, Glasgow Davey, Paxman & Co, (Colchester) Ltd	180, 5ft 38, 1ft 7, 0ft	469	2 sets 4 SCSA each 12cyl 7"X7½"	Forth Ferries Ltd, 1950-1954	Ex Admiralty LCT (4) 895-50 Converted by James Lamont & Co, Pt. Glasgow 1950 To Timblo, Irmados, Ltda, Goa, India 1954 Renamed HEMELATA 1954
Iron PS	FLYING FISH	1882	J. T. Eltringham South Shields J. P. Rennoldson Re-engined 1907 Hepple & Sons	116, 0ft 19, 6ft 10, 3ft	151	1) L 1cyl 38"X56" 75hp 2) NE&B '07 2eng. each L 1cyl 30"X45" 76nhp	J. S. Wilson 10/10/1906-3/2/1919 Wilson Executors 3/2/1919-30/9/1919	Ex Clyde Shipping Co, Glasgow 1882 J. Siddell, Sunderland 1882 F. Downs, Sunderland 1887 S. Chisholm, Sunderland 1894 T. L. Devlin, Granton 1900 To Leith Salvage & Towage Co, Leith 1919 C. Duncan & Sons, Middlesborough 1947 Broken up 1951

Type	Name	Date Built	Shipbuilder Place of Business Engine Builder	Length Breadth Depth	Gross Tons	Engine's Horse-Power	Forth Owners and Dates	Other Career and Dates
Iron PS	FORFARSHIRE	1861	Gourlay Brothers Dundee Gourlay Brothers	120. 5ft 20. 1ft 6. 7ft	115	SD 2cyl 22"X36" 40rhp NB '04	J.S. Wilson 20/10/1893-3/2/1919 Wilson Executors 5/2/1919-30/9/1919 Leith Salvage & Towage Co, 30/9/1919-21/3/1922	Ex Scottish Central Railway, Dundee 1861 Caledonian Railway, Dundee 1865 Dundee Harbour Trustees, Dundee 1873 Broken up Registry closed 21/3/1922
Wood PS	FORTH	1837	J. Duncanson Alloa Maxton	105. 1ft 15. 7ft 8. 5ft	122 144		Alloa, Stirling & Kincardine SB Co, 1837-1/7/1842	Woman Bust Figurehead, one mast Lengthened 6/1841 - 116. 6ftX 8. 8ft Main mast added 8/1841 To St. Petersburg, Russia W. Brandt & Co 1842
Iron PS	FORTH	1846	Hawarden Iron Co Hawarden, Flint	144. 4ft 26. 9ft 10. 4ft	210	SO 2cyl 44"X39" 120nhp NB '47, '53, '68	E&NR 2/1847-1/8/1849 EP&DR 1/8/1849-1862 NBR 1862-17/12/1879	Initially ordered by John Gladstone Full Female Figurehead Saloon fitted 1858 To S. M. Smart, Leith 1879 Broken up Registry closed 21/6/1880
Wood & Iron PS	FORTH	1855	S. & H. Morton Leith	137. 7ft 19. 5ft 8. 0ft	138	1cyl 46"X44" 70hp	Anstruther & Leith SS Co, 1856-1875	To H. Morton, Leith Machinery removed and used as a coal hulk by the London & Edinburgh Shipping Co. Registry closed 11/12/1885
Iron PS	FORTH	1884	J. T. Eltringham South Shields J. P. Rennoldson	108. 7ft 18. 6ft 9. 7ft	129	L 1cyl 36"X54" 80nhp	Forth Towing Co, 16/4/1892-22/11/1895 Grangemouth & Forth Towing Co, 22/11/1895-12/1923	Ex FLYING OWL Clyde Shipping Co, Glasgow 1884 Broken up at Alloa 1923
Wood TSMV	FORTH LADY	1947	-	112ft	126		John Hall (Cruises) Ltd, 1948-1950 Forth Ferries Ltd, 1950-1954	Ex Admiralty launch Converted by Vosper Ltd, Portsmouth 1948 Originally named ROYAL FORTH LADY but prefix quickly dropped Converted to yacht 1954
Wood PS	FURY	1857	- N. Shields	81ft 17ft 9ft	69	30hp	Chartered to J. Davidson & Co, for Fleet Visit 1860	Owned by J. Tweedy, North Shields
Iron & Steel PS	FUSILIER	1888	McArthur & Co Paisley Hutson & Corbett	202. 0ft 21. 6ft 8. 1ft	260	D 1cyl 49"X60" 142nhp NB '28 (made'02)	Redcliffe Shipping Co 7/1934-1935	Ex D. MacBrayne, W. Highland services 1888 To Cambrian Shipping Co, Blackpool 1935 Renamed LADY ORME 1935 Orme's Cruising Co, Ltd, Llandudno 1936 Renamed CRESTAWAVE 1936 Sold for scrapping 10/1939
Wood PS	GARIBALDI	1864	- Shields	83. 1ft 17. 9ft 9. 1ft	73	L 1cyl 34hp	G. Jamieson, Scott & Isabelle Stoker 4/5/1867-29/4/1870 G. Jamieson, J. Kerr, J. & T. Stoker 29/4/1870-11/5/1870	Ex Helen Stoker & G. Jamieson, Leith 1864 Sunk off the May Island 11/5/ 1870
Iron PS	GLADSTONE	1875	J. T. Eltringham S. Shields J. P. Rennoldson	118. 0ft 19. 8ft 10. 4ft	157	L 1cyl 40"X54" 95nhp	J. Henderson & J. McKean 28/5/1883-27/1/1890 Gave cruises at Czar's Visit 1896	Ex FLYING METEOR, Clyde Shipping Co, Glasgow 1875 Owned Sunderland 1882 Renamed GLADSTONE 1882 To F. Warren, Dundee Renamed COMMODORE 1890 Stranded and wrecked at St. Andrew's 11/12/1896
Wood PS	GLENALBYN	1834	Scott & Co Greenock	121. 3ft 19. 4ft 12. 6ft	200	165hp	General Shipping Co, 1838-1841 Gave Charity Cruise 9/1843 Chartered by Leith & Dundee SP Co 1844	Ex Glenalbyn SP Co, Glasgow 1834 North British SN Co, Glasgow 1837 On Berwick on Tweed service 1838-1841 To Hull & Leith SP Co, Hull 1841 W. & C. L, Ringrose, Hull 1854 Wrecked at mouth of River Maas 3/1856

Type	Name	Date Built	Shipbuilder Place of Business Engine Builder	Length Breadth Depth	Gross Tons	Engine's Horse-Power	Forth Owners and Dates	Other Career and Dates
Steel TSMV	GLENFINNAN	1944	- Davey, Paxman & Co, (Colchester Ltd)	180. 5ft 38. 1ft 7. 0ft	468	2 sets 4 SCSA each 12cyl 7"X7¾".	Forth Ferries Ltd, 1950-1954	Ex Admiralty LCT (4) 1048-50 Converted by James Lamont & Co, Pt. Glasgow 1950 To Timblo, Irmados, Ltda, Goa, India 1954 Renamed PRACAXA Lost 8/1955
Wood PS	GOLIAH	1852	John Bell North Shields	74. 5ft 15. 1ft 8. 8ft	23		MacGregor & Galloway 13/10/1853-1/2/1871	Ex M. Wharrier, North Shields 1852 To G. Jamieson, Leith 1871 Vessel unseaworthy Registry closed 8/1/1879
Iron PS	GRANTON	1844	J. B. Maxton & Co Leith J. B. Maxton & Co	126ft 20ft 9ft			John Gladstone & the Duke of Buccleuch 1844-1/1/1847 E&NR 1/1/1847-1/8/1849 EP&DR 1/8/1849-3/1856	To R. Cook & J. Inkster, Leith 1856 Engines removed and converted to schooner Coal hulk at Leith 7/1886
Iron PS	GRAPPLER	1884	J. T. Eltringham South Shields J. P. Rennoldson	80. 5ft 17. 6ft 9. 2ft	102	L 1cyl 32½"X50" 55hp	J. S. Wilson 25/8/1896-8/7/1911	Ex Cardiff & S. Shields 1884 To J. W. Davies, Liverpool 1911 R. Reynolds, Birkenhead 1916 Reynolds Executors, Birkenhead 1925 Broken up Registry closed 9/12/1953
PS	HARMONY						On charter to J. Davidson & Co for Fleet Visit 1863	
Iron PS	HEATHER BELL	1858	J. & G. Thomson Govan J. & G. Thomson	135. 5ft 18. 1ft 8. 3ft	152	SO. 2cyl	Used at Fleet Visit 1860	Owned by Christall, Gray & Bateson, Wick
PS	HELEN MACGREGOR						Andrew Greig 1850-1851	Newhaven-Aberdour & Kirkcaldy ferry 1850-1851
Wood PS	HERCULES	1853	J. Downey Jnr N. Shields	78. 0ft 15. 6ft 8. 6ft	63		Used at Fleet Visit 1860	Owned by Dundee, Perth & London Shipping Co, Dundee
PS	HERO						Andrew Greig 1851-1852	Newhaven-Aberdour & Kirkcaldy ferry 1851-1852
Steel PS	HIGHLAND QUEEN	1912	Earle's Co Ltd, Hull Earle's Co Ltd	195. 0ft 31. 1ft 8. 7ft	508	CD 2cyl 25"X48" X45"	Redcliffe Shipping Co 1935-12/1936	Ex BROCKLESBY, Great Central Railway, Hull 1912 LNER, Hull 1923 To German shipbreakers 12/1936
Steel	HOPE	1905	Mackay Brothers Alloa Aitchison-Blair & Co, Clydebank	63. 0ft 23. 1ft 4. 9ft		2-C each 7"&14" X10"	J. C. , J. &P. C. McLeod 22/8/1905-27/8/1921 P. C. McLeod 27/8/1921-25/1/1935 McLeod executes 25/1/1935-13/5/1940	To Royal Burgh of Inverness 1940 Vessel no longer in use Registry closed 17/1/1947
-	HURWORTH	-	-	-	-	-	-	See CONQUEROR
Wood PS	INTEGRITY	1870	R. Stobbs North Shields J. P. Almond	85. 2ft 17. 6ft 9. 2ft	80	L 1cyl 31½"X48" 32hp	James Dykes 17/5/1872-12/9/1874	Ex -, North Shields 1870 Reg. Leith 1872 transferred to Dundee 3/1874 To J. Dent Jnr, Blyth 1874
Wood PS	ISLE OF ARRAN	1838	- Port Glasgow	129. 5ft 20. 1ft 8. 9ft	129	1cyl 60hp	John Johnson 17/5/1860-2/12/1861	Ex Isle of Arran Shipping Co, Ardrossan 1838 To J. Mackillican, Invergordon 1861 Reeve & Clarke, Norwich 1861
-	ISLE OF SKYE	-	-	-	-	-	-	See FAIR MAID
Iron SS	IVANHOE	1850	- St. Peters Northumberland	137. 2ft 21. 0ft 12. 0ft	229	2cyl 70hp	Used at Fleet Visit 1860	Male Figurehead Owned by Cox, McGregor & Lindsay, Leith
Iron PS	JAMES COX	1875	C. Mitchell & Co Low Walker R. Stephenson	68. 5ft 10. 9ft 4. 5ft	24	2cyl SO 15hp	NBR 9/2/1879-30/6/1884	Ex CROW, Tyne ferry 1876 On Tay ferry 1879-1884 To J. Constant, London 1884 W. C. Middleton, Sligo Renamed BOWMORE 1887 Wrecked, Rosses Pt. 11/1½ 1904
Wood PS	JAMES WATT	1821	J. & C. Wood Port Glasgow		143	150hp	London & Edinburgh SP Co 1821-1836	To General Steam Navigation Co, London 1836 Broken up in 1840's

K

Type	Name	Date Built	Shipbuilder Place of Business Engine Builder	Length Breadth Depth	Gross Tons	Engine's Horse-Power	Forth Owners and Dates	Other Career and Dates
	JANE						James Falshaw 1852-2/1855 Scottish Central Railway 2/1855-8/1855	Alloa ferry
Iron TSS/ PS	JOHN BEAUMONT	1876	J. Key & Sons Kinghorn 1) J. Key & Sons 2) Lees, Anderson & Co	125, 4ft 24, 3ft 7, 4ft	165	1) S 2cyl 18"X18" 35hp 2) CD2cyl 17"&32" X36" 45hp	NBR 12/2/1877-26/4/1890 John Arthur 26/4/1890-31/5/1894	Propeller at each end Re-engined & converted to paddle steamer 1879 To T. W. Ward, Sheffield 1894 G. Esseyou, Manchester 1898 Borgas Bergamli, Smyrna 1899 Turkish Hamidie SS Co, Constantinople 1899 Renamed GUL BAHTCHE
Iron PS	JOHN STIRLING	1876	J. Key & Sons Kinghorn J. Key & Sons	190, 3ft 27, 0ft 10, 5ft	427	SO 2cyl 54"X51" 250hp NB'85	NBR 8/5/1876-8/6/1892	To J. C. Glover, Edinburgh 1892 Chartered for Manchester Ship Canal cruises 1894 T. W. Ward, Sheffield 1899 C. H. Sunderman, Dordrecht, Holland 1899 Broken up 1900
Iron PS	JUPITER	1876	J. & T. Eltringham South Shields Hepple & Co	96, 1ft 17, 9ft 9, 2ft	102	L 1cyl 33½"X50" 40hp	J. & G. Mackay & G. Pederson 3/7/1876-29/3/1886 Executors of above 29/3/1886-21/10/1891 Grangemouth Towing Co 21/10/1891-1895 Grangemouth & Forth Towing Co 1895-24/6/1914	To O. W. Jewels, Blyth 1914 R. Bell, Blyth 1919
Iron PS	KINLOCH	1865	A. & J. Inglis Glasgow A. & J. Inglis	216, 0ft 36, 2ft 8, 6ft	585	2-SD2cyl (1cr) 42"X48" 260hp NB'78	NBR 1865-11/11/1890	Train ferry To W. T. MacLennan, Glasgow 1890 T. C. Glover, Edinburgh 1892 Broken up 1892
Wood PS	LADY OF THE LAKE	1815	John Gray Kincardine James Cook	70, 3ft 16, 2ft 10, 9ft	83	SL 22hp	Stirling Steamboat Co 1815-1826 Alloa, Stirling & Kincardine Steamboat Co, 1826-1831	Chartered to Germans and ran on River Elbe 4/1816-10/1817 To T. Cookson, Leith 1831 Lost 1843
	LCT 895	-	-	-	-	-	-	See FLORA MACDONALD
Iron PS	LEVIATHAN	1849	R. Napier & Sons Glasgow R. Napier & Sons	167, 0ft 34, 6ft 8, 5ft	399	2 St each 1cyl 56"X42" 210hp NB '57, '65	EP&DR 7/2/1850-1862 NBR 1862-1890	Train ferry To W. T. MacLennan, Glasgow 1890 T. C. Glover, Edinburgh 1892 Broken up 1892
	LION						1828-1833	Newhaven-Grangemouth service At Broughty Ferry 1836
Wood PS	LION	1847	- East Jarrow	68, 6ft 14, 5ft 8, 0ft		28hp	Stoker executors (Hall, Fryar & Oliver) 13/6/1853-1860's	Ex Waterman, Johnson, Ioliff, N. Shields 1847 Used at fleet visit 1860 Remained at Leith till c'1865 as a tug
Wood PS	LIONESS	1858	- North Shields	80ft 16ft 8ft	60		Chartered by J. Davidson & Co for Fleet Visit 1860	Owned by A. Grant, North Shields
Wood PS	LIVINGSTON	1876	Woodhave & Johnston North Shields T. R. Scott & Co	94, 1ft 18, 8ft 9, 5ft	96	L 1cyl 34, 3/8"X 51" 39hp	Henry Burrell 19/6/1876-18/6/1881 Henderson & McKean 18/6/1881-2/6/1890	To J. Dent, Newcastle 1890 O. W. Jewels, Blyth 1906 Lost 26/9/1913
Wood PS	LOCHRYAN	1830	- Dumbarton		127		? 1843	On Leith-Newcastle run
Iron SS	LONDON	1856	Gourlay Brothers Dundee Gourlay Brothers	209ft 28ft 16ft	622	C 2cyl 47"X77" X48" 460hp	Used at Fleet Visit 1860	Owned by Dundee, Perth & London Shipping Co
Iron PS	LORD ABERDOUR	1866	Aitken & Mansel Glasgow Aitken & Mansel	142, 0ft 20, 1ft 6, 9ft	130 later 368	SO2cyl 30"X36" 60hp NB'75	MacGregor & Galloway 28/5/1866-25/4/1869 D. R. MacGregor 25/4/1869-19/1/1874 John Kidd 19/1/1874-19/8/1875 Kidd & Newton 19/8/1875-24/12/1875 Kidd & Watson 24/12/1875-29/4/1880 Forth River SS Co, 29/4/1880-9/4/1886 Galloway Saloon SP Co, 9/4/1886-1900	M. P. Galloway appointed manager 22/12/1875 Broken up by Hawthorns at Granton Registry closed 18/12/1900
PS.	LORD DUNDAS						Forth & Clyde Canal Co, 1831	On Glasgow-Grangemouth-Alloa service

Type	Name	Date Built	Shipbuilder Place of Business Engine Builder	Length Breadth Depth	Gross Tons	Engine's Horse- Power	Forth Owners and Dates	Other Career and Dates
Iron PS	LORD ELGIN	1876	Richardson, Duck & Co Stockton-on-Tees T. Richardson	160.0ft 20.0ft 6.8ft	203	CD2cyl 22"&42" X42" 75nhp	John Kidd 3/1876-29/4/1880 Kidd Executors 29/4/1880-14/5/1881	Two masts M. P. Galloway - manager To Bournemouth, Swanage & Poole SP Co 1881 Southampton, Isle of Wight & South of England Royal Mail SP Co 1909 Broken up 1955
Iron PS	LORD ELGIN	1867	G. Robinson & Co Cork, Ireland	96.0ft 18.1ft 9.8ft	107	L 1cyl 36"X54" 50hp	J.S. Wilson 14/4/1898-4/5/1900	Ex Queenstown Towing Co, Cork 1867 W. Liddell, Glasgow 1882 Ardrossan Harbour Co, Ardrossan 1887 Broken up Registry closed 4/5/1900
SS	LORD ERSKINE	1886	W. Drake Grangemouth A. Bryce, Alloa	33.4ft 10.0ft 4.0ft	7	2cyl 5hp	A. McLeod 16/6/1887-18/5/1911	Alloa ferry steamer Broken up
Iron PS	LORD MAR	1876	Richardson, Duck & Co Stockton-on-Tees T. Richardson	160.0ft 20.0ft 6.8ft	203	CD2cyl 22"&42" X42" 75nhp	John Kidd 4/1876-31/3/1879	Two masts M. P. Galloway - manager To F. Youle, London 1879 M. J. D'America, Pernambuco, Brazil 1879 Arrived at Maccio, Brazil 6/1879
Iron PS	LORD MORTON	1883	S. & H. Morton Leith S. & H. Morton	169.9ft 20.3ft 7.1ft (Len'00 181.9ft)	186 ('00:- 220)	D 1cyl 45"X54" 85hp NB'00	Forth River SS Co 1883-9/4/1886 Galloway Saloon SP Co 9/4/1886-12/8/1917	Requisitioned by Admiralty 28/8/1916 Purchased by Admiralty 12/8/1917 Converted to hospital carrier HC7 Blown up in White Sea, Russia 24/9/1919
Iron PS	LOUISE CRAWSHAW	1860	- St. Peter's Quay	96ft 14ft 7ft	50	24hp	Used at Fleet Visit 1860	Owned by J. Rodgerson, Newcastle Broken up 1898
Wood PS	MAID OF ISLAY	1815	John Hunter Port Glasgow James Cook	100.4ft 15.9ft 9.0ft	79	20hp	On Dundee-Leith service 1836	Ex WATERLOO Renamed 1825 Lengthened 1826 Ex Clyde, Irish & West Highland services
Wood PS	MAID OF LEVEN	1839	- Paisley	123.3ft 19.0ft 8.0ft	76		John Gladstone 6/9/1844-19/7/1853 Chartered to E&NR/EP&DR 1/1/1847-19/7/1853 W.J. Anderson 8/3/1854-?	Ex Dumbarton Steamboat Co, Dumbarton 1839 Granton-Burntisland ferry 1844-1853 Also on Tay from 1849 To C. Watson, Middlesborough 1853 Leith-Largo ferry 1854 To Paris, Registration cancelled 1857
PS	MANCHESTER						Forth & Clyde Canal Co, 1832	On Glasgow-Grangemouth-Alloa service
Steel PMV	MARY QUEEN OF SCOTS	1949	W. Denny & Brothers Dumbarton Crossley Brothers	149.0ft 28.1ft 6.9ft	230	2 eng each SA 8cyls 180X 230mm Chain Drive	W. Denny & Brothers Ltd 3/1950-6/9/1964	To Caledonian SP Co Broken up, Inverkeithing 1965
Iron PS	MAY	1870	- Low Walker	78.0ft 16.1ft 8.4ft	67	27hp	James Dykes 20/4/1870-23/3/1872	To J. Stevenson, Stettin, Prussia 1872 W. Chisholm, North Shields 1879
Wood &Iron PS	MAY	1875	Hepple & Co S. Shields Hepple & Co	116.3ft 18.8ft 9.4ft	123	L 1cyl 32½"X54" 42hp	James Dykes 27/5/1875-27/11/1879	To J. Wood, Bridlington 1879 Great Eastern Railway, Lowestoft 1893 Broken up? 1901
Steel PS	MIDLOTHIAN	1881	Ramage & Ferguson Leith J. Key & Sons	262.6ft 40.3ft 10.0ft	920	2-CD 2cyl(1cr) 35"&70" X60" 920nhp	NBR 21/12/1881-9/10/1890	Train ferry To W. T. MacLennan, Glasgow 1890 Bank of Vera Cruz, London 1891 G. Hume Ltd, London 1892 J.W. Cooper & J. Greig, London 1893 Ibo Syndicate Ltd, London 1895 Ibo Investment Trust, London 1897

Type	Name	Date Built	Shipbuilder Place of Business Engine Builder	Length Breadth Depth	Gross Tons	Engine's Horse-Power	Forth Owners and Dates	Other Career and Dates
Steel PS	MIDLOTHIAN (continued)							G.E. Borrage, London 1897 T.W. Ward, Sheffield 1897 Broken up in Sweden 10/1898
Wood PS	MODERN ATHENS	1836	J. Adamson Broughty Ferry P. Borrie	115.0ft 10.5ft 10.8ft	201	SL 2cyl 43"X48" 120hp	Dundee & Leith SP Co 1836-1846	On Dundee service 1836-1846 To J. Ramsay, Isle of Islay 1846 Tod & McGregor, Glasgow 1849 J.A. Bremner Liverpool 1852 F. McMahon & J. Cragg, Liverpool 1854 Reduced to a hulk 1864
Wood PS	MONARCH	1833	Wigram & Green Blackwall	204ft 30ft	816	220hp	Used at Queen Victoria's Visit 1842	Owned by General Steam Navigation Co
Wood PS	MONTROSE	1862	T. Hepple & Co Low Walker	73ft 15ft 8ft	51	20hp	Adam Gibb (on charter) 1865 (advertised as LORD ABERDOUR)	J.&F. Batey, Newcastle 5/1862 T. Hepple, Newcastle 4/1869 To Russian owners 10/1869
Iron SS	MORE VANE	1869	- Birkenhead	71.8ft 11.2ft 5.1ft	32		Dr. R.Bruce 1886	Yacht Owned by Dr. Bruce until sold to Norwegians 1891
Wood PS	MORNING STAR	1815	Ralph Rae Kincardine D. Napier ('18)	87.5ft 14.7ft 8.5ft	106	NB '16 NE&B '18	Alloa Steamboat Co 1815-1826 Alloa,Stirling&Kincardine SB Co 1826-1836 Musselburgh & Fisherrow SP Co 1836 Alloa & Leith SP Co 1836-1856	Two masts, no bowsprit On Alloa & Stirling service 1815-1836 On Berwick on Tweed service 1836 Luggage boat 1837-1855 Broken up Registry closed 12/1/1856
Wood PS	NEPTUNE	1837	- Shields		174	100hp	Shields & Newcastle General SN Co 1839	On Hull-Leith/Dundee services
Wood PS	NEWCASTLE	1824	- Newcastle		42		- 1824	On Newhaven-Newcastle service
Wood PS	NEWHAVEN	1847			259	80hp	Aberdeen, Leith & Clyde Shipping Co 1849-1851	Ex Brighton & Continental SP Co 1847 On Aberdeen service 1849-1851 To W. Geoch, London 1851 Registry closed 1856
Iron PS	NEW UNDAUNTED	1882	- Cobham Island	94.5ft 14.2ft 7.0ft	65	45rhp	John Arthur 1/1889-1893	Ex JUMBO, R.J. Blyth, Great Yarmouth 1882 G.J. Spicer, Gravesend 1888 To W. Black, Inverness 1893 Renamed NESS QUEEN 1893 Broken up Registry closed 4/1906
Wood PS	NIGHT WATCH	1857	- North Shields	84ft 17ft 9ft	72	35hp	Chartered to A. Boyne & Co for Fleet Visit 1860	Owned by R. Lister, Sunderland
Wood PS	NORTHERN YACHT	1835	R. Barclay Glasgow R. Napier	116.6ft 16.7ft 9.2ft	99		On Newhaven-Dundee service 1836-1837	Ex T.&R. Barclay, Glasgow 1835 To Shields & Newcastle SN Co 1837 Wrecked, All hands lost 1837
Iron PS	NYMPH	1851	T. Vernon Liverpool	113.3ft 17.9ft 7.8ft	91	45nhp	John Croall 6/1/1865-31/5/1872 Croall Executors 31/5/1872-21/7/1873 NBR 21/7/1873-24/3/1885	Ex J. Crippen & W.R. Forster, Liverpool 1851 T.F.&R. Netherington, Liverpool 1856 Broken up
Wood PS	OLGA						Used at Fleet Visit 1860	
Wood PS	PEARL	1865	- Cobble Dean South Shields	82.7ft 17.4ft 9.1ft	73 ('81:- 63)	40hp	MacGregor & Galloway 6/5/1865-14/7/1873 MacGregor & Carter 14/7/1873-11/10/1876 Burns, Chisholm, McBryde, Lawson & McGlashlan 20/10/1876-5/6/1888	To MacGregor & M.P. Galloway, Leith 1876 J.N. Campbell, Leith 1876 To W. Malcolm, Bo'ness 1888 W. Taylor, Grangemouth 1890 J. Hogg, Bo'ness 1890 Forth Towing Co, Grangemouth 1892 Broken up Registry closed 19/1/1897
PS	PERO GOMEZ	1869	- Low Walker T. Hepple & Co	88.0ft 17.6ft 9.1ft	96	L 1cyl	J.S. Wilson 4/3/1902-3/2/1919 Wilson Executors 3/2/1919-27/3/1919	Ex R. Rosser, Swansea 1869 - , Leith 1900 To R.L.C. Baister, Sunderland 1919 Converted to a lighter Registry closed 14/6/1922

Type	Name	Date Built	Shipbuilder Place of Business Engine Builder	Length Breadth Depth	Gross Tons	Engine's Horse-Power	Forth Owners and Dates	Other Career and Dates
Wood PS	PILOT	1860	North Shields	82ft 16ft 9ft	67	30hp	On charter to MacGregor & Galloway 1860	Owned by W. T. Turnbull & M. Wheldon, Howdon, Co. Durham 1860 To J.B. Calleman, Sunderland by 1865 J.W. Snowdon, Sunderland by 1882 Broken up 1892
Wood PS	POWERFUL	1865	Cobble Dean South Shields	89, 9ft 18, 2ft 9, 5ft	89	34hp	Laidlaw, Steedman & Carnie 7/3/1866-28/10/1866 Steedman, Hanson & Dykes 28/10/1866-28/10/1870 Steedman, Hanson & Mudie 28/10/1870-8/6/1875	Ex W. Best, South Shields To Wilson, Mudie & Hanson, North Shields 1875 Oats, Mudie & Hanson, North Shields 1875 Oats, North Shields 1875 J. Minto, Leith 1888 A, A. T. Moyes, Alloa 1893 Broken up Registry closed 4/10/1898 (Under Danish flag - 11/72-4/77?)
Iron SS	PRINCE ALFRED	1860	Smith & Rodgers Glasgow	212, 2ft 28, 1ft 16, 0ft	695	170nhp	Used at Fleet Visit 1860	Owned by London & Edinburgh Shipping Co Wrecked 13/1/1861
Iron PS	PRINCE OF WALES	1845	J. Reid & Co Port Glasgow R. Napier	130, 3ft 21, 1ft 7, 9ft	154	80hp NB'57	Alloa, Stirling & Kincardine SB Co 1845-1873 W. Beveridge 1874-1875	To W. Chalmers & D. McIntyre, Glasgow 1876 D. Dewar, Glasgow 1877 Russian Owners 4/1879
Iron PS	PRINCESS OF WALES	1866	Aitken & Mansel Glasgow J. Aitkin & Co	142, 6ft 16, 7ft 6, 8ft	112	SO 2cyl 30"X42" 60rhp	M. Brydie 26/10/1881-25/5/1883 J. Cran 25/5/1883-19/4/1884 W. Beveridge 19/4/1884-1/5/1885	Ex Loch Lomond 1866 To J. Beveridge, Alloa 1885 W.B. Ritchie, Dundee 1886 Dundee, Perth & Newburgh SB Co 1886 J.C. Forbes, Dundee 1886 T.S. Blakeney, Dundee 1887 J.K. Henderson, Dundee 1887 D. Nicoll, Dundee 1892 The Dundee Pleasure Boat Co 1894 W.T. Rogers, Dundee 1896 Renamed ALBION 1896 Dundee & Perth Passenger SB Co 1899 J. Brodie, Dundee 1901 North Eastern Passenger Steamers Ltd, Newcastle1901 G. Martin, Dundee 1903 Renamed SHAMROCK 1903 E.W.C. Abbott, London 1909 The Foreland SB Co, London 1910 French owners Registry closed 27/8/1912
Steel PS	PRINCESS OF WALES	1896	R. Craggs & Sons Middlesborough Jamieson & MacColl	139, 6ft 18, 1ft 7, 5ft	163	CD 2cyl 21"&39" X30" 65rhp	Stanley Butler SS Co 1926-1927	Ex Medway SP Co, Rochester 1896 New Medway SP Co, Rochester 1919 To New Medway SP Co, Rochester 1927 T.W. Ward for scrapping 10/ 1928
Iron PS	QUEEN	1840	J. & C. Carmichael Dundee	106, 5ft 20, 2ft 10, 2ft	182	70hp	Trustees of Fife & Midlothian Ferry 1840-1844 Kirkcaldy, Leith & Newhaven Ferry SB Co 1844-31/3/1849	Two masts, Female Bust Figurehead, bowspit To J. Nicholson, Liverpool 1849 J. Newton, Liverpool 1854 W. & T. Jollith, Liverpool 1858 Broken up 1859
Iron PS	QUEEN	1845	W. Simpson & Co Aberdeen	183, 0ft 26, 0ft 14, 5ft	602	260nhp	Aberdeen, Leith & Clyde Shipping Co 1845-1857	On Aberdeen service 1845-1857 Wrecked on Carr Rocks, Fife 19/4/1857
Wood PS	QUEEN MARGARET	1821	Menzies & Co Leith		100		Queensferry Trustees 9/1821-1841	Queensferry ferry boat Lengthened by 7ft 1828
Steel PEMV	QUEEN MARGARET	1934	W. Denny & Brothers Dumbarton Davey, Paxman & Co	149, 0ft 28, 1ft 6, 9ft	228	2-each 4 SCSA 8 cyls 6½"X10" driving electric generators	W. Denny & Brothers 1/3/1934-6/9/1964	To Caledonian SP Co 1954 Broken up at Inverkeithing 1965
Wood PS	QUENTIN DURWARD	1823	S. Rankin Leith	101ft 16ft 9ft	78	52hp	Leith & Dundee SP Co 1824-1826 (on charter to Edinburgh, Glasgow & Leith Shipping Co 1826)	Ex R. Ogilvie & G. Crichton, Leith 1823 To L. Christensen, Copenhagen 1827 Renamed DANIA 1827

Type	Name	Date Built	Shipbuilder Place of Business Engine Builder	Length Breadth Depth	Gross Tons	Engine's Horse-Power	Forth Owners and Dates	Other Career and Dates
Wood PS	QUENTIN DURWARD (continued)							M.W. Saas, Copenhagen 1828 C. Den, Ostend Engines removed 1840 Broken up - Copenhagen 1841
Wood PS	RAPID						- 1826-1829 Dysart, Leith, Edinburgh, Leven & Largo SP Co 1830-1831	On Newhaven-Newcastle service 1826-27 On Newhaven-Dundee service 1828-29 On Newhaven-Largo service 1830-31 Destroyed by fire at Dysart 1/4/1831
Steel PS	REDGAUNTLET	1895	Barclay, Curle & Co Glasgow Barclay, Curle & Co	215.0ft 22.0ft 7.4ft	277	D 1cyl 53"X72" 183nhp	Galloway Saloon SP Co 3/1909-12/8/1917	Ex NBR, Clyde services 1895 Requisitioned by Admiralty 23/5/1916 Purchased by Admiralty 12/8/1917 To Cie, de Navires Olivier, Oran, Algeria 1921 Registry closed 1934
Iron PS	RENOWN	1881	Hughes & Drives N. Shields Baird & Barnsley	94.0ft 18.3ft 9.8ft	94	L 1cyl 33½"X50" 36hp	Used at Czars visit 1896	Tay excursion tug Owned by F. Warren, J.&P. Stephenson & G. Legg, North Shields & Dundee
Wood PS	RESOLUTE	1859	- N. Shields	83ft 16ft 9ft	67	35hp	Used at Fleet Visit 1860	Later owned in London
Wood PS	RIFLEMAN.	1860	- N. Shields	77ft 15ft 8ft	53	28hp	Used at Fleet Visit 1860	Owned by J.&J. Scope, Newcastle
Wood PS	RIVAL	1847	- Middlesborough	84.7ft 13.3ft 7.0ft	14NT		On charter to A. Greig 1849 for Newhaven-Aberdour ferry	Owned by J. Stoker, Shields
Wood PS	ROB ROY						On charter to A. Greig 1850	Newhaven-Aberdour & Kirkcaldy ferry 1850
Wood PS	ROBERT AIREY						Used at Fleet Visit 1860	
Wood PS	ROBERT BRUCE	1856	T. Adamson Alloa	69.0ft 17.1ft 7.6ft	53	L 1cyl 27hp	On charter to J. Davidson & Co Fleet Visits 1860 & 1863	Owned by T. Adamson, Alloa
Iron PS	ROBERT NAPIER	1850	R. Napier & Sons Glasgow R. Napier & Sons	129.6ft 23.8ft 8.5ft	243 (216 '76)	SO 2cyl 42"X42" 120hp	EP&DR 1850-1862 NBR 1862-1888 NB '56 '68	Train ferry Usually on Tay 1851-53, 1868-80 Re-measured 1876 - 137.4ftX24.4ftX8.5ft Used on Tay Bridge reconstruction from 1880 Converted to coal hulk. Registry closed 20/12/1888
Wood PS	ROBERT SCOTT	1862	- Shields	82.3ft 17.7ft 8.9ft	77	2L-each 1cyl 33hp	MacGregor & Galloway 29/10/1862-27/7/1864	Ex R.&H. Scott, S.Shields 1862 To T.M. Tennant, Leith 1864 Foundered near Anstruther 7/1864
Wood PS	ROBERT STEPHENSON	1860	- N. Shields	84.0ft 17.5ft 9.0ft	74	40hp	Chartered by War Office to view Inchkeith Bombardment 1884	Owned by Duke of Buccleuch, Granton
Wood PS	ROBERT SUTHERLAND						Chartered by A. Boyne & Co for Fleet Visit 1860	
Wood PS	ROBERT THE BRUCE	1823		76ft			Subscribers to the Alloa Steam Ferry 1823-c'1840	Catamaran design
Steel PEMV	ROBERT THE BRUCE	1934	W. Denny & Brothers Dumbarton Davey, Paxman & Co	149.0ft 28.1ft 6.9ft	228	2 -each 4SCSA 8cyls 6½"X10" driving electric generators	W. Denny & Brothers 1934-6/9/1964	First electrically welded ship To Caledonian SP Co Broken up, Bo'ness 1965
Steel TSS	ROSLIN CASTLE	1906	Hawthorn & Co Leith Hawthorn & Co	185.0ft 26.1ft 8.8ft	392	2 -each 3cyl 14", 22" & 35" X 18" 183nhp	Galloway Saloon SP Co 5/1906-3/1908	To Admiralty Renamed HMS NIMBLE 1908 Stationed at Shearness till 1922, then Chatham Lloyds Albert Yacht & Motor Packet Service, Southampton 1948 Broken up, Belgium 1949
Wood PS	ROTHESAY	1831	J. Lang Dumbarton D. Napier	93.6ft 15.0ft 8.9ft	58	-	1834-1836 Dundee & Leith SP Co 17/6/1836-11/3/1839	Bowspit, male bust figurehead, two masts Ex J. McKinnon, Glasgow 1831 C. McKenzie, Glasgow 1834 On Dundee & Montrose services 1834-1839

Type	Name	Date Built	Shipbuilder Place of Business Engine Builder	Length Breadth Depth	Gross Tons	Engine's Horse-Power	Forth Owners and Dates	Other Career and Dates
Wood PS	ROTHESAY (continued)							To Liquidator and thence to Hull 1840
-	ROYAL FORTH LADY	-	-	-	-	-	-	See FORTH LADY
Wood PS	ROYAL GEORGE	1830	W. Hawks, Son & Co, Gateshead	69.4ft 15.4ft		40hp	Chartered by A. Greig 1830 for Largo ferry	Figurehead Owned by Will Hawks, Son & Co, Gateshead
Steel TSMV	ROYAL LADY	1938	J. Crown & Sons Sunderland Crossley Brothers	137.8ft 25.2ft 9.0ft	245		John Hall (Cruises) Ltd 1947	Ex NEW ROYAL LADY J. Round, Scarborough To General Steam Navigation Co, London Renamed CRESTED EAGLE 1948 Malta, renamed IMPERIAL EAGLE 1957
Iron PS	ROYAL NORMAN	1881	J.T. Eltringham S. Shields J.P. Rennoldson	108.0ft 18.6ft 9.8ft	144	L 1cyl 37"X54" 70nhp	J.W. Wilson 21/3/1896-3/2/1919 Wilson Executors 3/2/1919-6/10/1919	Ex D. Blakey, Sunderland 1881 Sharp Brothers, Cardiff 1884 To Leith Salvage & Towage Co, Leith 1919 Broken up Registry closed 19/1/1926
Wood PS	ROYAL TAR	1836	Tod & McGregor Glasgow Tod & McGregor	125.7ft 16.6ft 8.8ft	79		A. Greig 1843-1845 Edinburgh & Dundee SP Co 1845-1846	Ex J. Henderson & A. McKellar, Glasgow 1836 Newhaven-Largo ferry 1843-1846 To H. Nicholls, Eastham, Liverpool 1846 W. Hillian, Liverpool 1847 J. Crippen & W.H. Forster Liverpool 1850
-	ROYAL TAY LADY	-	-	-	-	-	-	See ULSTER LADY
Iron PS	ROYAL VICTORIA	1838	Barr & McNab Paisley	106.8ft 13.2ft 7.3ft	58		Chartered by 1) Alloa, Stirling & Kincardine SB Co 1850 2) Hall & Stoker 1853	Former Clyde & West Highland steamer, owned by the Dundee & Perth SP Co On Stirling service 1850 On Kirkcaldy ferry 1853
Wood PS	RUBY	1862	R. Stobbs Cobble Dean	75.3ft 15.7ft 8.4ft	56	23hp	MacGregor & Galloway 8/4/1862-14/7/1863 MacGregor & Carter 14/7/1873-2/12/1876	To W. MacGregor & M.P. Galloway, Leith 1876 W. Beveridge, Alloa 1876 J. Bibb, Alloa 1885 A. Adam & T. Moyes, Alloa 1889 Broken up Registry closed 15/10/1898
Iron PS	RUNNER	1886	J.T. Eltringham S. Shields J.P. Rennoldson	108.0ft 18.6ft 9.7ft	131	L 1cyl 36"X54" 80nhp	Grangemouth & Forth Towing Co 3/7/1912-8/3/1927	Ex Clyde Shipping Co, FLYING SCOTSMAN 1886 A. MacKinnon, Greenock renamed CHAMPION 1897 Renamed RUNNER 6/7/1916 Broken up at Alloa 1927
Wood PS	ST. GEORGE	1836	J.H. Ritchie & J. Wood Port Glasgow Neilson	101.0ft 16.9ft 8.3ft	78	48hp	A. Greig 8/1831-1843	Ex Lochgoil SB Co, Glasgow 1826 Newhaven-Largo ferry 1831-1843 Machinery used in Clyde steamer PRINCE - built 1846
Iron SS	ST. NICHOLAS	1871	J.C. Lawrie & Co Glasgow J. Howden & Co	227.5ft 27.2ft 14.6ft	787	C 2cyl 35¾"&60" X39" 200nhp	Used on Duke of Edinburgh's visit 1881	Owned by the North of Scotland Orkney & Shetland SN Co
Wood PS	SAMSON	1840	- S. Shields	88.3ft 16.8ft 9.9ft			Chartered by 1) Andrew Greig 1852 for Aberdour ferry 2) John Davidson & Co for Fleet Visits 1860 & 1863	Owners Dundee Perth & London Shipping Co, Dundee 1840 - , Aberdeen 1843 Hall, Stoker & Oliver, Leith 1853 Broken up Registry closed 9/11/1870
Iron PS	SAMSON	1857	- S. Shields	81.8ft 18.3ft 9.5ft	82	L 2cyl 40hp	Used at Fleet Visit 1860	Owned by Dundee, Perth & London Shipping Co, Dundee

Type	Name	Date Built	Shipbuilder Place of Business Engine Builder	Length, Breadth Depth	Gross Tons	Engine's Horse-Power	Forth Owners and Dates	Other Career and Dates
Wood PS	SCOTTISH MAID						Chartered to J. Davidson & Co for Fleet Visits 1860 & 1863	Owned by C. Stein, Alloa
Wood PS	SEA KING	1869	- N. Shields T. R. Scott & Co	96.2ft 18.4ft 9.8ft	24	46hp	J. Moodie, Jnr & J.S. Wilson 27/2/1884-18/11/1886 D.&J.S. Wilson 18/11/1886-24/1/1890 J.S. & Eliz. Wilson 24/1/1890-22/8/1892	Ex - , Greenock 1875 Lost Certificate cancelled 22/8/1892
Wood PS	SIR WILLIAM WALLACE	1816	J. & C. Wood & James Barclay Port Glasgow Greenhead Foundry	81.5ft 16.2ft 8.9ft	93	20hp	Fife & Midlothian Ferry Trustees 14/7/1820-18/1/1825	Ex LORD NELSON, J. Wilson, Glasgow 1816 Rebuilt & lengthened J. Cook, Glasgow 1820 Newhaven-Pettycur & Kirkcaldy ferry 1820-1825 Wrecked at Burntisland 18/1/1825
Steel PMV	SIR WILLIAM WALLACE	1956	W. Denny & Brothers Dumbarton Crossley Brothers	159.2ft 30.0ft 7.9ft	277	2-each 2 SA 4cyl 179mmX 229mm	W. Denny & Brothers 3/1956-6/9/1964	To Caledonian SP Co 1964 D. Arnold, Southampton 1965 - , Holland 1965 - , Basle, Switzerland 1969
Steel PS	SLIEVE BEARNAGH	1894	J. & G. Thomson Clydebank J. & G. Thomson	225.6ft 26.1ft 8.6ft	383	CD2cyl 25", 54" X54" 178nhp	Used by Nicols on Forth 1914	Belfast & County Down Railway 1894 D.&J. Nicol, Dundee 1912 Admiralty 10/1917 Converted to Hospital Carrier HC5 1/1919 Broken up Inverkeithing 1923
Wood PS	SOVEREIGN	1836	- Port Glasgow	158.7ft 24.7ft 13.5ft	417	240hp	Aberdeen, Leith & Clyde Shipping Co 1836-1865	On Aberdeen service 1836-1865 To J.B. Adam, Aberdeen 1865 F.T. Barry, London 1865 E. Kearnon, Arklow, Ireland 1872 (Engines removed 1872) Wrecked - Muros, Spain 7/1/1901
Wood PS	STAR	1821			90			Stated in Government White Paper 1822 as built for Forth ferry Not traced
Wood PS	STAR	1847	- N. Shields	67.5ft 14.5ft 8.1ft	51	25hp	A. Greig 1854-1855 (Newhaven-Aberdour ferry)	Ex To Fraser, Hall & Nicholson, Leith 1855 P. Matthews, Glasgow 1864
Iron PS	STAR	1849	Tod & McGregor Glasgow Tod & McGregor	156.0ft 17.9ft 8.4ft	95	St.1cyl 100nhp	J.D. Luke 1860	From & To Largs, Millport & Arran SB Co, Glasgow To American Civil War Blockade Running 1863 At Nassau, Bahamas till 1920's
	STELLA						Used at Fleet Visit 1860	
Wood PS	STIRLING CASTLE	1814	- Greenock and Kincardine				Stirling Steamboat Co (H. Bell) 1814-1820	Pseudonym 'THE STIRLING STEAMBOAT' Transferred to Caledonian Canal 1820 Wrecked near Ardgour, Argyll 1/1828
Wood PS	STIRLING CASTLE	1826	J. Wood Port Glasgow R. Napier	98.0ft 16.0ft 8.0ft	93	SL 40hp	Alloa, Stirling & Kincardine SB Co 1826-1842 J.C. Todd 1842-10/4/1845 Anstruther & Leith SS Co 10/4/1845-16/12/1848 Alloa & Leith SP Co 16/12/1848-12/4/1866	Male Bust Figurehead, two masts Major repair 1835 - 90.7ftX32.5ftX8.2ft On Stirling service 1826-1842 On Anstruther service 1845-1848 Luggage boat 1848-1866 To D. Sneddon, Alloa 1866 J. Priestley & J. Gash, Aberdeen 1871 Broken up 6/1872
Steel PS	STIRLING CASTLE	1884	S. & H. Morton Leith S. & H. Morton	160.3ft 20.1ft 6.9ft	160	D1cyl 43"X54" 80nhp	Forth River SS Co 1884-9/4/1886 Galloway Saloon SP Co 9/4/1886-24/5/1898	To Idarei Masusieh, Constantinople 1898 Renamed ANATOLI 1898 Admin. De Nav a vapeur Ottoman, Constantinople - 1912 Lost during first world war ,
Steel PS	STIRLING CASTLE	1899	J. Scott & Co Kinghorn J. Scott & Co	170.0ft 24.2ft 7.6ft	271	CD 3cyl 22"&48" X54" Discon' 141nhp	Galloway Saloon SP Co 7/10/1899-13/5/1907	To Southampton, Isle of Wight & South of England Royal Mail SP Co 1907 Requisitioned by Admiralty 1916

Type	Name	Date Built	Shipbuilder Place of Business Engine Builder	Length Breadth Depth	Gross Tons	Engine's Horse-Power	Forth Owners and Dates	Other Career and Dates
Steel PS	STIRLING CASTLE (continued)							Sunk by mine off Malta 26/9/1916
Wood PS	STOKERS	1859	- N. Shields	84.7ft 16.5ft 8.8ft	69	L1cyl 30hp	E.E. Oliver 7/7/1859-14/9/1863	Wrecked near Ardrossan, Firth of Clyde 1863
Wood PS	STORM KING	1866		89ft 18ft 10ft	88	35hp	Jamieson & Stoker c'1868-c'1873	To J. Batey, Newcastle 1874
Wood MV	SUNBEAM						J. Bremner 5/1937-12/1939	Ex Largs, Firth of Clyde Alloa Ferry Boat 1937-1939
Iron PS	SUPERB	1839	J. Lang Dumbarton R. Napier	122.0ft 20.0ft 8.1ft	70		Alloa, Stirling & Kincardine SB Co (Never delivered)	Rejected, as she drew too much water To R. Napier, Glasgow 1839 - , Liverpool 1847 Sunk in collision in Mersey 1847
Wood PS	SURPRISE	1821	J. Lang Dumbarton		120		Edinburgh, Glasgow Leith & London Shipping Co 1/1821-1/2/1822	Newhaven-east Fife ferry 1821-1822 Wrecked near Leven 1822
Steel PS	TANTALLON CASTLE	1887	S. & H. Morton Leith S. & H. Morton	190.0ft 21.1ft ('95 7.7ft Lengthened '95- 202-0	240 ('95 257)	D 1cyl 45"X60" 100nhp ('95-126) NB '95	Galloway Saloon SP Co 1887-25/4/1898	To Jdarei Massousieh, Constantinople 1898 Renamed FERAH 1898 Admin. de Nav a Vapeur Ottoman, Constantinople 1912 Lost during first World War
Steel PS	TANTALLON CASTLE	1899	J. Scott & Co Kinghorn J. Scott & Co	210.0ft 25.1ft 8.4ft	333	CD2cyl 27"&58" X54" 1,100IHP	Galloway Saloon SP Co 6/5/1899-4/1901	To J. Lee, Shoreham 1901 Renamed SUSSEX BELLE 1901 Sussex SP Co 1902 Colwyn Bay & Liverpool SS Co 1903 Renamed RHOS COLWYN 1903 Barry & Bristol Channel SS Co 1905 Renamed WESTONIA 1905 Red Funnel Line, Barry 1907 Bristol Channel Passenger Boats 1910 P.&A. Campbell, Bristol 1912 Renamed TINTERN 1912 Caminhos de Ferra du Sule Sueste, Lisbon, Portugal Renamed ALENTEJO 1912 Deleted from register 1927
Wood PS	TARTAR	1843	J. Dowey N. Shields	76.6ft 15.4ft 8.3ft	21		Hall, Nicholson & Oliver 1/5/1854-12/4/1856	Ex To - , Stockton 1856 Broken up 10/1895
Wood PS	TARTAR	1861	- N. Shields	80.7ft 16.8ft 9.0ft	70	30hp	Chartered by J. Davidson & Co for Fleet Visit 1861	Owned by W. Nicholson, Leith
Wood SS	THANE	1858	J. Scott Inverkeithing	109ft 19ft 10ft	153	20hp	Used at Fleet Visit 1860	Owned by J. Scott, Bo'ness
Wood PS	THANE OF FIFE	1821	J. & C. Wood Port Glasgow	91.5ft 16.6ft 11.0ft	129	50hp	Fife & Midlothian Ferry Trustees 1821-14/4/1846	Short bowspit, billet head, two masts To T. Ness, Leith 1846 L. Rose, Leith 1846 Converted to sailing schooner 1846 A. Meighan & M. Walker, Glasgow 1852 J.&W. Walker, Glasgow 1853 J. Laurence, Melbourne, Australia 1856 A. Locking, Sydney, Australia 1860 J.H. Hall & J. Abbot, Auckland, New Zealand 1867 Wrecked at Fiji 17/9/1868
Iron PS	THANE OF FIFE	1847	Miller & Ravenshill Blackwall Miller & Ravenshill	141.0ft 18.9ft 9.7ft	171	SO2cyls 34"X33" 70nhp NB'54, '62, '81	E&NR 1847-1/8/1849 EP&DR 1/8/1849-1862 NBR 1862-11/11/1890	Man Bust Figurehead Saloon fitted 1854 Usually on Tay ferry 1879 To W.T. MacLennan, Glasgow 1890 O.S.S. Piper, Port Talbot, Glamorgan 1891 J. Rosmussen & Racine, Stavanger 1892 Renamed TURISTEN 1892 Sank in Bergen fairway 14/9/1893

Type	Name	Date Built	Shipbuilder Place of Business Engine Builder	Length Breadth Depth	Gross Tons	Engine's Horse-Power	Forth Owners and Dates	Other Career and Dates
Iron PS	THE EARL	1872	Redhead, Softly & Co S. Shields Redhead, Softly & Co	114.9ft 19.6ft 10.0ft	144	2-L each 1cyl 90"X54" 60nhp	J.S. Wilson 24/9/1914-3/2/1919 Wilson Executors 3/2/1919-6/10/1919	Ex SUSSEX G. Haslip, London 1872 R. Holland, London 1887 W. Gray & Co, Hull 1889 Ardrossan Harbour Co Renamed WELSHMAN 1892 Renamed THE EARL 1914 To Leith Salvage & Towage Co, Leith 1919 Broken up Registry closed 16/3/1928
Steel TSMV	THE SECOND SNARK	1938	W. Denny & Brothers Dumbarton Gleniffer Engines		50		W. Denny & Brothers 1960-11/1963 Brown Brothers & Co 11/1963-29/5/1969	Ex W. Denny & Brothers Shipyard tug/tender 1938 To Clyde Marine Motoring, Greenock 1969 Re-engined 1972
Wood PS	THOMAS & MARY	1857	James Jack Middlesborough	83.7ft 17.5ft 8.3ft	77		J.S. Wilson 3/5/1894-31/7/1896	Ex -, North Shields 1857 R. Gilmore & J.S. Wilson, Burntisland 1893 Broken up Registry closed 23/11/1896
Wood PS	TOURIST	1821	James Brown Perth	119ft 23ft 13ft	257		Leith & Aberdeen SY Co 1821-1823	To London & Edinburgh SP Co, London 1823 J.S. Brickwood, London 1832 General Steam Navigation Co, London 1832 Stranded at Gt.Yarmouth 16/11/1854
Iron PS	TRANSIT	1864	Hepple & Co Low Walker Hepple & Co	99ft 18ft 8ft	83	L 1cyl 40hp NE & B '77	M. Brydie (on charter) 1881	Ex Isle of Wight Ferry Co, London 1864 Bournemouth SP Co 1878 W.&C. P. Hepple, S. Shields 1880 To J.A. Platt, London 11/1881 J.P. Lawson, London 3/1892 W. MacGregor & H. Blair, Leith 3/1894 Broken up 12/1908
Iron PS	TRIDENT	1841	Wigram & Green Blackwall	193ft 29ft 19ft	971	280hp	Used at Queen Victoria's Visit 1842	Owned by General Steam Navigation Co, London
Wood PS	TUG	1817	J. Wood & Co Port Glasgow McArthur		95	2 engines each 16hp NB '25	Edinburgh, Glasgow & Leith Shipping Co 1817-c'1821 London, Leith, Edinburgh & Glasgow Shipping Co c'1821-8/1838	On Newhaven-Grangemouth service 1817-1838 To D. Jackson, Leith 1838 Converted to a sailing craft 1838 A. McNaughton, Leith 1844 Suffren, Jnr, Belfast 1845 J. Watt, Maryport 1848 Broken up Registry closed 12/1876
Wood PS	TULLIALLAN CASTLE	1828	Gray Kincardine	80ft 16ft		34nhp	- 1828-c'1835 Subscribers to the Alloa Steam Ferry c'1835-?	Initially on Kincardine ferry
Wood PS	TYNE	1857	- Newcastle	84ft 16ft 9ft	68		Chartered to J. Davidson & Co for Fleet Visit 1860	Owned by W. Nelson, Newcastle
Wood TSMV	ULSTER LADY	194?	-	112ft	126		John Hall (Cruises) Ltd 1948-1950 Forth Ferries Ltd 1951-1954	Ex Admiralty launch Converted by Vosper Ltd, Portsmouth 1948. Named ROYAL TAY LADY then TAY LADY. On Tay & Forth Renamed ULSTER LADY 1949. Used on Belfast Lough 1949. Clyde 1950 To Regent Diesels Ltd, Leeds 1954 Broken up 10/1955
Wood PS	VELOCITY	1821	W. Denny Dumbarton Greenhead Foundry Co	112ft* 20ft 12ft	260	2 engines each 20hp	Aberdeen & Leith SY Co 1821-1826 Aberdeen, Leith & Clyde Shipping Co 1826-1844	To Aberdeen & Newcastle SN Co 1844 Wrecked on Aberdeen pier 25/10/1848 *After lengthening 1844

Type	Name	Date Built	Shipbuilder Place of Business Engine Builder	Length Breadth Depth	Gross Tons	Engine's Horse-Power	Forth Owners and Dates	Other Career and Dates
Wood PS	VENUS	1868	Brodie & Maxwell N. Shields W. Scott & Co	81.9ft 17.6ft 9.1ft	74	L 1cyl 33hp	J.S. Wilson 11/3/1890-8/12/1902	Ex Feely, Pederson & Strong, Grangemouth 1868 - , N.Shields 1879 Broken up Registry closed 6/12/1902
Wood PS	VICTOR	1852	R. & R. Stobbs N. Shields	71.1ft 14.7ft 7.7ft	60		Chartered by J. Davidson & Co for Fleet Visit 1860	Owned by Stoker, Jamieson & Stobbs, Leith
Wood PS	VICTORIA	1834	Hunter & Dow Glasgow	89.9ft 16.0ft 8.3ft	76 ('37-91)	34hp	Alloa, Stirling & Kincardine SB Co 1834-1845	Woman Bust Figurehead Len. '37 97.3'X15.3'X7' Lost on voyage to Copenhagen 1845
Iron PS	VICTORIA	1858	R. Napier & Sons Glasgow R. Napier	135.8ft 15.6ft 6.7ft	92	SO 2cyl 40nhp	Alloa, Stirling & Kincardine SB Co 26/5/1858-13/5/1874 James Neill 13/5/1874-25/1/1877	To Tranmere Ferry Co, Liverpool 1877 Broken up 1881
Wood PS	VICTORY	1825	Howden Pans, Northumberland	74.0ft 17.2ft 8.4ft	47		Cookson, Ogilvie, Hogg & Sanderson 1826-9/2/1831 Dysart, Leith, Edinburgh Leven & Largo SP Co 9/2/1831-13/3/1832	Male Bust Figurehead, two masts On Newhaven-Largo ferry 1826-1832 To J. Pletts & E. Elstor, North Shields 1832 - , Newcastle 1836
Wood PS	VICTORY	1844	R.Dixson S. Shore, Durham	91ft 14ft 9ft	93	40hp	Aberdeen, Leith & Clyde Shipping Co 1847-1860	Ex J. Strong, Middlesborough 1844 On Aberdeen service 1847-1860 To E. Johnson, Liverpool 1860 Broken up 1871
Wood PS	WALKER	1857	- Low Walker	83ft 16ft 9ft	66	30hp	Chartered by J. Davidson & Co for Fleet Visit 1860	Tyne tug. Owned by 1862 by J. Dodds, Middlesborough
Wood PS	WATERWITCH	1840	- Shields		12	14hp	Used at Queen Victoria's visit 1842	
Iron PS	WEMYSS CASTLE	1872	H. Murray & Co Port Glasgow D. Rowan	180.0ft 18.2ft 6.8ft	172	SO 2cyl 35"X54" 85rhp NB '90	Galloway Saloon SP Co 25/6/1891-4/1906	Ex GARELOCH, NBR Clyde services 1872 Broken up 1906
Iron PS	WILLIAM ADAM	1838	Menzies & Co Leith J.B. Maxton & Co		49	40hp	Queensferry Trustees 1838-9/1864	To NBR, Burntisland 1864 R. Slimmon, Leith 11/1866
Wood PS	WILLIAM INNES						- 1825	On Newhaven-Newcastle service 1825
Iron PS	WILLIAM MUIR	1879	J. Key & Sons Kinghorn 1) J. Key & Sons 2) Ramage & Ferguson	174.1ft 24.1ft 10.7ft	364 412	1)SO 2cyl 46"X48" 225nhp NB'92 2)NE&B'10 CD 2cyl 28"&52"X 60" 174nhp	NBR 29/7/1879-1/1/1923 LNER 1/1/1923-7/5/1937	Broken up at Charlestown 1937
Wood PS	WILLIAM SCOTT	1868	Brodie & Maxwell N. Shields W. Scott & Co	82.7ft 17.3ft 9.1ft	78	L 1cyl 32½"X48" 35hp	James Dykes 18/4/1872-13/11/1874	Ex - , N. Shields 1868 Transferred to Dundee 12/3/1874 To Hudson, Dalgleish, Pallister, Gascoigne & Heaton, North Shields 1874
Iron PS	WINDSOR CASTLE	1838	Tod & McGregor Glasgow Tod & McGregor	130.0ft 16.5ft	151	St. 1cyl SO hp	Edinburgh & Dundee SP Co 8/1844-1/10/1844	Ex Castle SP Co, Glasgow 1838 Glasgow Castle, SP Co, Glasgow 1842 Wrecked after hitting Carr beacon 1/10/1844
Iron PS	WOOLWICH	1890	The Thames Iron Works & SB Co Blackwall T.A. Young & Sons	100.0ft 20.6ft 8.0ft	148 ('09 129)	SO 2cyl 25"X30" 40nhp	J.S. Wilson 9/1908-3/2/1919 Wilson Executors 3/2/1919-6/10/1919 Leith Salvage & Towage Co 6/10/1919-8/10/1923	Ex Great Eastern Railway, Woolwich 1890 Broken up Registry closed 8/10/1923

Type	Name	Date Built	Shipbuilder Place of Business Engine Builder	Length Breadth Depth	Gross Tons	Engine's Horse-Power	Forth Owners and Dates	Other Career and Dates
Iron PS	XANTHO	1848	Denny & Co Dumbarton Penn & Son, London	106.8ft 16.8ft 8.4ft (116ft'71)	62 ('56- 97) (110- '71)	60hp	Anstruther & Leith SS Co 4/1848-1858 MacGregor & Galloway 1858-1859	Demi-woman figurehead, two masts To W. Strong, Scarborough 1860 J. Anderson & J. Barnes, Wick 1864 J. McGann, Wick 1870 R. Stewart, Glasgow 1871 Sunk-Port Gregory, W. Australia 17/11/1872
PS								On Kincardine ferry 1830's- 1853
PS							Subscribers to Alloa Steam Ferry 1830's-1845 Edinburgh & Glasgow Rail- way 12/1845-1852	Pronounced unseaworthy 1852
Iron PS	FLYING BAT	1884	J.T. Eltringham South Shields J.P. Rennoldson	108.3ft 18.9ft 9.7ft	130	L.1cyl 36"X36" 80nhp	J.C.I. & I. McLeod 6/6/1896-14/6/1915	Ex Clyde Shipping Co., Glasgow 1884 To Nicholson Steam Tug & Salvage Co., Leith 1913 Leith Salvage & Towage Co., Leith 1919 Broken up Registry closed 2/10/1923
Steel TSS	THANE OF FIFE	1910	Cammell, Laird & Co Birkenhead Cammell, Laird & Co	152.3ft 38.6ft 10.9ft	457	2-Teach 3cyl 16", 24" &41"X 21" 207nhp	LNER 10/1936-1947	Ex SNOWDROP County Borough of Wallasey 1910 Requisitioned for naval tender duties 1940 Broken up, Alloa 1947

Bibliography

Coton, R. H. *A Decline of the Paddle Steamer* 1971

Donaldson, G. *Northwards by Sea* 1966

Duckworth, C. L. D., and Langmuir, G. E. *Clyde and Other Coastal Steamers* 1939

Duckworth, C. L. D., and Langmuir, G. E. *Clyde River and Other Steamers* 1938, 1947 and 1972

Duckworth, C. L. D., and Langmuir, G. E. *Railway and Other Steamers* 1948

Duckworth, C. L. D., and Langmuir, G. E. *West Coast Steamers* 1953, 1966

Duckworth, C. L. D., and Langmuir, G. E. *West Highland Steamers* 1936, 1950 and 1967

Erskine, Ex Bailie *Glimpses of Modern Burntisland* 1920

Grimshaw, G. *British Pleasure Steamers 1920-1939* 1939

Hammond, R. *The Forth Bridge and its Builders* 1964

Mason, J. *The Story of the Water Passage at Queensferry* 1964
Paterson, A. J. S. *The Golden Years of the Clyde Passenger Steamer*
1969
Thomas, J. *The North British Railway, Volume One* 1969
Thomas, J. *The Tay Bridge Disaster* 1971
Williamson, J. *The Clyde Passenger Steamer* 1904

The minute books and other records of the relevant railway
companies and the Galloway Saloon Steam Packet Company in
the Scottish Record Office have also been consulted, as have
newspapers of the areas concerned. Among miscellaneous records
consulted have been the ship registration books for Forth ports.

Author's Notes and Acknowledgements

In writing this book I have been fortunate in having access to
three main sources of material; the railway archives held in the
Scottish Record Office, Edinburgh; the ship registration books
for all the ports in the area; and the local newspaper files.

I thank George Barbour and Andrew Broom of the Scottish
Record Office, for having made much material available and
suggested several avenues of research which proved extremely
fruitful. Information derived therefrom, and transcripts of crown
copyright material in the Scottish Record Office appear by
permission of the Keeper of the Records of Scotland.

The ship registrars have requested to remain anonymous but
their valuable assistance cannot go unrecorded and yielded considerable information. G. H. Somner has also assisted with
historical information, both from the London registration records
and from the records of the World Ship Society. I have also to
record my thanks and appreciation to the staff of the National
Library for Scotland, Edinburgh; the Edinburgh Room and
Leith sections of the Edinburgh Public Libraries; and the
Bo'ness, Stirling, and Dundee libraries for their assistance over a
long period, chiefly in the field of newspaper research. I also

gratefully acknowledge the reading facilities provided by the *Grangemouth Advertiser* and information supplied by the Grangemouth and Forth Towing Co Ltd.

I acknowledge with pleasure the assistance of G. E. Langmuir, in allowing unrestricted access to his photographic collection, also Aberdeen University Library for a print from the G. W. Wilson collection, and Messrs E. R. Yerbury & Sons for a print from the Balmain collection. Messrs W. Barrie, J. Stirling Gray, I. H. Shannon, E. A. Wilson and Mrs Sclater for assistance with photographs, some of which were used in the preparation of line drawings.

The artistic talents of Eric Berryman are self evident, but all the more remarkable when it is appreciated that he only paid a brief visit to the Forth area, and was in Singapore when he made the drawings.

I also record my appreciation to various individuals who have provided information: Tom McBain of South Queensferry who was my first contact and gave valuable leads; W. Barrie with valuable scrap books containing articles by the late J. H. Sutherland, better known to news readers of the 1930s as 'John o' Leith', William Bell of Grangemouth for information on the *Comet*, J. Bremner of Alloa for notes on that ferry and a thrilling trip by small boat through the Windings; the McLauchlans of Aberdour for local details and for obtaining the Passage poster from their neighbour Mrs Maxwell; also John Penny, master of *Sir William Wallace* for details of his ship, James Watson for details of diagonal engines and I. Robertson for a copy of *Glimpses of Modern Burntisland*. Not least of all, I have great pleasure in thanking John Thomas, for having encouraged me in the first instance to undertake this work and for his invaluable advice and help at various stages. A number of typists are also thanked for their work, as is Ben Bickerton for his work on the photographic plates. My wife and family are sincerely thanked for organising their lives around this book and encouraging its writing.

The detailed research has been a pleasure to me, giving an enlightening insight into the history of the Forth. It has made me realise that the river I grew up beside was once a throbbing artery for local passenger shipping, and that many important events took place on its waters and around its shores.

I. B.

Index

(Illustrations in italic type)

Aberdour, 14–22, 25–9, 32, 39–42, 65–6, *68*, 73–4, 79, 81, 84–90, 112, 116, *119*, 139, 141, 144
Aitken, Thomas, 28, 35–6, 40–1, 62–4, 73, 116
Alloa (and ferry), 5, 8, 22–32, 51, 57, 65–6, 70–3, 76, 79, 84, 87–9, 93, 108, 111, 136, 140, 142, 144
Alloa Bridge, 9–11, 31–4, 51, 57
Anstruther, 16, 22–5, 35, 39, 65, 75, 85, 136, 139, 143–4
Arthur, Captain John, 46, 58, 133

Bass Rock, 13, 17, 21–2, 26–9, 35, 39, 42–3, 65, 75–6, 85–6, 89, 109, 115, 139–40, 142–3
Bell Rock, 27, 29, 39, 42, 140
Berwick, 13, 43, 73, 139
Beveridge, Walter, 23, 30–4
Blackness, 27, 42, 85–7
Board of Trade, 37, 41, 48, 52–3, 71, 76, 97
Bo'ness, 5, 8, 12, 25, 32–3, 65, 69–71, 75–7, 87–8, 91, 93, 105, 112, 142, 144
British Railways, 96, 105
Brown Bros & Co Ltd, 105–6
Brydie, Matthew, 29–31
Buccleuch, Duke of, 13, 47, 78, 116
Buckhaven, 40, 43
Burntisland (and ferry), 19–20, 47–51, *50*, 53–9, 66, 71, 78–9, 81, 85, 87, 91–4, 97–9, 105, 113, 116–18, 122, 125, 128, 142, 144

Caledonian Railway, 51
Carr, North Light, 65, 75, 112
Charlestown, 12, 37, 46, 65, 69–70, 84, 144
Charters, 43, 46, 71, 73, 76, 87, 144
Coach Tours, 11, 32, 39, 104
Cockenzie, 17, 105–6
Cramond, 85
Croall, Robert, 32–3, 35–6, 40
Culross (& Blair), 32, 70–1, 84

Denny, Wm & Bros., 90–1, 96, 100, 104, 129, 134
Dunbar, 13, 20, 35, 40, 65

Dundee, 19–20, 22, 27, 29, 34, 39, 43, 53, 62, 108, 111–12, 136, 139–40
Dunmore, 11, 16, 23, 86
Dykes, James, 19–20
Dysart, 11, 16, 23, 86

Electric light (on ships), 38–9, 42, 74
Elie, 19, 22–9, 35–7, 39–40, 42–3, 70, 75, 81, 86, 139–40, 142–3
Evening cruises, 35, 39, 42, 74, 84, 86, 88–9, 100–1, 139–43
Eyemouth, 13

Farne Islands, 39, 62
Fidra, 35, 85, 142
Fisherrow, 13
Flory boats, 7–8, 17, 37, 81, 87
Forth Bridge, 34–6, 40–2, 46, 53, 55, 57–8, 70–3, 75–6, 84–9, 96, *102*, 113, 115, 139–41
Forth Ferries Ltd, 98–9, 134

Galloway, M. P., 6, 19, 24–8, 30, 32–6, 40–1, 45, 62–4, 77
Galloway Saloon SP Co, 36–46, 60–6, *61*, *67–8*, 73–9, 81, 87, *101*, 113–16, 126–8, 132–3, 141–3
Gibb, Adam, 16
Grangemouth, 7–8, 28, 35, 42, 51, 71–3, 75–6, 81, 84–5, 87–9, 91, 116
Grangemouth & Forth Towing Co, 46, 72–3, 81, 84–5, 87–90, *119*, 132
Granton, 12–13, 23–5, 47–51, 53, 59, 62, 79, 81, 85, 88–9, 92, 94–5, 98–9, *101*, 104–5, 108–9, 111–12, 116–17, 137–8
Greig, Andrew, 12–13
Grierson, Henry, 73, 75–7

Hall, John, 94–8, 111, *120*, 134
Henderson & McKean, 46

Inchcolm, 15–16, 19, 30, 82, 85–7, 95, 98, 104–5, 115, *120*, 139
Inchkeith, 21, 27, 30, 35, 38, 42, 65, 70, 76, 84–5, 111, 113–14, 139–40
Inverkeithing, 15–16, 22, 105, 116, 140

Jamieson, George, 6, 20–2, 30–1
34–5, *49*, 70, 132

Kidd family, 24–8, 35–6, 40
Kincardine, 5, 8, 12, 23–5, 33, 36, 65,
70, 75, 84, 93, 142
Kirk, Deas, & Co, 85, 116, 134
Kirkcaldy, 7, 12, 15–7, 19, 22, 28, 30,
35–7, 42–3, 65, 70, 73, 76–7, 84,
86–8, 108–9, 112, 116, 136, 139, 142
Kirkcaldy Towing Co, 73, 77, 134

LNER, 83–4, 90–1, 96, 131–2
Largo, 12, 15, 23, 36–9, 43, 65–6, 142
Leith, 5–6, 10, 13, 15–36, 40–4, 57,
62, 71, 73–6, 81, 84–9, *101*, 107–16,
119, 136, 139–44
Leith Salvage & Towage Co, 82, 132
Leven, 11, 15, 23, 77
Limekilns (& Brucehaven), 25, 70

MacGregor & Galloway, 15–19, 24,
132
McLeod (Alloa), 51, 69, 73, 93, 132
Mar & Kellie, Earl of, 51, 81
Matthew & Mathieson, 29–30, 34, 132,
139–40
May Island, 17, 19, 21, 25, 27, 29–30,
34–5, 39, 42, 67, 70, 75, 85–86, 96,
139, 140, 143–4
Methil, 43, 65, 75–7, 81, 95, 142–3
Morton, Earl of, 16–17, 77

NBR, 37, 40–1, 47–59, *50*, 63–6, 73–8,
81–2, 114, 131–2, 135
Navigation limits, 7
Newhaven, 8, 12–3, *49*, 107–8, 111,
137
Nicol, D. & J., 77–9, 132
North Berwick, 19–22, 25–6, 30, 35–6,
40, 42, *68*, 75, 81, 85, 89, 140,
142–3

Perth, 27, 34

Pettycur, 43
Pittenweem, 23, 136
Portobello, 7, 13, 17, 19, 35–7, 39–40,
42–4, 62–3, 65, 67, 70–1, 73, 75–6,
79, 85, 89–90, 114–15, 142–3

Queensferry (and ferry), 5, 7, 9, 11,
20, 22, 28, 30, 32, 34–6, 39–43, 48,
51–3, 55, 57–61, 65–6, 69–71, 75,
77–85, 90–1, 93, 96–7, 99–105, *102*,
107–13, 116–17, 127, 129, 138–41

Rail/Steamer tickets, 43
Redcliffe Shipping Co, 88, 95, 134
Rosyth, 64, 71, 73, 79–80, 85, 89

St Abb's Head, 29, 39
St Andrews, 17, 22, 43, 75, 139, 143
SMT Co, 71–2, 79, 85, 111, 116
Ship repairers, 41, 44–5, 52, 54–5,
58–62, 66, 74–5
Sinkings, 20, 23, 53, 86, 112–13
Stanley-Butler SS Co, 86–7, 116, *119*,
134
Stirling, 5, 8, 12, 22–8, 30–5, 39, 42,
60–1, 70, 73, 77, 88–9, 108, 142, 144
Stirling SB Co, 23, 26, 30, 115
Stoker family, 15, 20
Sunday Steamers, 17, 20, 30, 34–5, 37,
42–3, 65–6, 73, 75, 84

Telescopic funnel, 10–11, 34, 38, 62
Tender duties, 43, 87, 91, 99–100, 103
Tide, 7–9, 39–40, 52, 76, 103–4, 127
Touting (custom of), 21, 30
Train ferries, 47–8, *50*, 53–9, 90,
117–18, 125

Wallace, Andrew, 32, 35–7, 39–41, 63
Watson, Anthony, 24, 28, 35–6, 40
Wilson (Bo'ness), 46, 58, 69–72, 81,
110, 116, 133, 144
Windings (of river), 5–9, 32, 65, 71,
72, 73, 76, 84, 142, 144